MERRY CROSS

Proud Child, Safer Child

A Handbook for Parents and Carers of Disabled Children

First published by The Women's Press Ltd, 1998
A member of the Namara Group
34 Great Sutton Street, London EC1V 0DX

British Library Cataloguing-in-Publication Data
A catalogue record for this book is available from the British Library.

ISBN 0 7043 4561 7

Typeset in Sabon 11/12 pt by FSH Ltd, London
Printed and bound in Great Britain by Cox & Wyman Ltd, Reading, Berkshire

This book is dedicated to all the disabled children who have so enriched my life, but particularly Nduku and Kazee; and also to the memory of my mother, who always dreamed of writing a book herself.

Contents

Acknowledgements

I'd like to take this opportunity to acknowledge the crucial role that the love I've received from my mother, father and sister has played in my life, and to thank my father, especially, for his rock-solid support.

My greatest thanks are due to all the disabled children who have shared their lives, experiences and their thinking with me. I've drawn heavily on what I've learnt from them in the writing of this book. Many thanks are due to all the parents who gave their time generously to provide such helpful comments on the first draft, some of whom can't be named (in order to protect the anonymity of their children), but who include Terry Smith and Kay Beadle. Particular thanks are due to Bharti Dhir for her help and guidance with the finer details of the last chapter. Thanks, too, to Ruth Marchant for her comments, suggestions and encouragement, and finally to my editor, Kirsty Dunseath, for easing a nervous first-time sole author through to publication.

Foreword

I am writing this book as a woman who was once a disabled child and who, still disabled, is now a mother of non-disabled children. I write as someone who has always loved children, particularly working with disabled children. I know the horrors of abuse and have listened to far too many disabled people telling their stories of abuse ever to be complacent about this issue again. The stories I have heard have been from people with sensory impairments, people with mobility impairments, people with complex impairments, people with behavioural problems and people with learning difficulties. Therefore this book is intended to be fully inclusive of parents and carers of children with any and all impairments, none more or less than any other. Equally I have listened to people from just about every racial and religious background, born in this country and born elsewhere. So I hope that this book will be useful for as diverse an audience as possible, no matter what the background, and no matter what the disability.

You may be raising or helping to raise one or more

disabled children. My hope is that this book will give you many ideas about how to set these children up with the highest self-esteem, feeling empowered to take on the many challenges that will come their way. It should also give you ideas for practical measures to improve their safety. Certainly my intention is always to equip, rather than to alarm you. Nevertheless this can be a distressing subject and it is best to acknowledge that fact. I have attempted to balance the need to alert readers to the risks that disabled children face with the desire to equip them with a myriad ways to reduce those risks. It is probably not possible to read from cover to cover without having to stop occasionally and deal with quite painful feelings. But if you are able to come back to the book and end up feeling better equipped to protect the children in your care, I will have succeeded in the delicate tightrope walk I have set myself.

Life for parents and carers of disabled children, for all the joys, is almost always complex and full of exhausting battles; most often we are thrown into this bewildering new world with little or no warning and, frequently, with far too little emotional support. Like all those entrusted with the care of children we muddle through, and do our best.

You may, however, be a professional, or perhaps a student, wanting to understand this area more. It is always important to bear in mind and appreciate the difficulties parents face. On the other hand, it is important not to forget that parents and carers of disabled children can also abuse. These men and women, contrary to the popular myth that they are all saints with the patience of Job, are absolutely ordinary people whose reactions to their not so ordinary task vary as much as humanity itself. Some rise to the occasion and surprise even themselves with their strength, determination and, above all, fierce love for their children. Most, guided by that love, stumble along like the rest of us, getting lots right, and lots wrong.

However, it is certainly true that more disabled children are abused by their parents (and other family members) than non-disabled children. The best and some of the most recent research suggests that disabled children are, on average, and across all four types of abuse (emotional, physical, sexual and neglect), almost twice as likely to be abused within their families as non-disabled children.[1] Too many parents neglect their children out of shame. Some scapegoat their disabled children for all their misfortunes and physically abuse them as well as constantly humiliating them. A small number will sexually abuse their own children, but probably abuse other children too. We also know, however, that disabled children are highly at risk of abuse in the many institutions in which they find themselves. This book then addresses itself to parents and carers who want to reduce the risk their children face to a minimum.

It is not the purpose of this book to dwell on research or statistics. It is not intended to be an academic study, but there is a bibliography at the end for those who want to know more.

There is no doubt that many of us find it extremely difficult to believe that disabled children need protecting from abuse – there is a widespread belief that no one would stoop so low. But if we look at society's increasing emphasis on detecting abnormality in foetuses, allowing abortion *up to term* should such an abnormality emerge, and encouraging the mother to have an abortion in that case, we should not be surprised. Considering how many mothers are told some version of 'It would have been better if your child had died at birth' or 'Never mind, you can give this one up for adoption and try for another', it is really not inconceivable that disabled children are at risk of abuse.

In 'Prenatal Testing and the Prevention of Impairment' Ruth Bailey says 'It could be argued that prenatal testing has in a sense institutionalised the fear of impairment and increased the value attached to non-disabled children.'[2] If there is increased value attached to the birth of non-disabled children, then there is decreased value attached to disabled children, and devalued children are always at risk.

Finally I am taking the liberty of talking about 'our children' throughout this book, when I mean disabled children, even though mine are not disabled. This is because I feel so strongly connected to disabled children and also because it is less clumsy than some other options.

Introduction

It is almost certain that anyone interested enough to pick up this book has some awareness of how vulnerable disabled children are. The main objective of *Proud Child, Safer Child*, then, is to help readers by suggesting ideas about how to build the child's self-esteem and how to promote the safest practices in ourselves and in those entrusted with disabled children's care. Along the way, however, we must have clarity about abuse and abusive practices.

Abuse is always about the misuse of a power imbalance, and one of the reasons that disabled children are so targeted for abuse is that there are more power imbalances available for exploitation in their lives. Thus it is possible to do anything to a child with whom, for example, nobody can (or does) communicate, safe in the knowledge that they will be unable to 'tell' others. It is easy to knock down even a fifteen-year-old lad if he wears calipers. It is easy to use silence to scare a blind child. We can socially exclude deaf children without even thinking about it, making them feel isolated and vulnerable. We can ensure that children who use an artificial communication system are silenced simply by removing their communication equipment. Children and adults who use wheelchairs are all too familiar with the problem of other people pushing them wherever and whenever they wish without even considering consulting the wheelchair user. Children with difficult behaviour are not likely to be believed. The list goes on . . .

Unfortunately the above do not constitute abuse officially. A report published by the National Commission of Enquiry into Child Protection suggested that the definition of abuse should be greatly broadened, but this has been dismissed almost out of hand by the powers that be.[1] So we are still stuck with the official categories and definitions of abuse. These are as follows and are taken from 'Working Together under the Children Act 1989'.[2]

Neglect   The persistent or severe neglect of any child, or the failure to protect a child from exposure to any kind of danger, including cold or starvation, or extreme failure to carry out important aspects of care, resulting in the significant impairment of the child's health or development, including non-organic failure to thrive.

Physical injury   Actual or likely physical injury to a child, or failure to prevent physical injury (or suffering) to a child including deliberate poisoning, suffocation and Munchausen's syndrome by proxy.[3]

Sexual Abuse   Actual or likely sexual exploitation of a child or adolescent. The child may be dependent and/or developmentally immature.

Emotional abuse   Actual or likely severe adverse effect on the emotional and behavioural development of a child caused by persistent or severe emotional ill-treatment or rejection. All abuse involves some emotional ill-treatment. This category should be used where it is the main or sole form of abuse.

It is important to point out that all I have written is directed towards helping protect our children from *all* kinds of abuse, not just sexual abuse. Although sexual abuse receives the most publicity, it is neither the only nor the most important type of abuse. Abuse of any kind at all is traumatic and destructive – a nightmare whose severity is not to be judged by others, because it is lived by the child.

What is abusive practice?

Abusive practice is any practice which is profoundly disrespectful of a person as a human being, even if it would not fall within the official categories of abuse recognised under the law. It is practice based on assumptions that are false and contemptuous. For instance, I was recently told about a local authority that had been vetting their foster carers. There was one family they were really uneasy about. But they were short of foster families, so instead of striking them off the list, they decided that only disabled children could be sent to this family! This is abusive practice at the institutional level and clearly based on the assumption that what happens to disabled children is less important than what happens to non-disabled children.

Or consider the language which often gets used in institutions and which will be discussed later in the book. It is abusive practice to call disabled children 'manuals' or 'SLDs' or 'feeders'. The assumption here is that the children don't have feelings like other children, whereas the reality is frequently that these children have no safe avenues for expressing those feelings.

It is abusive practice for a parent or carer to prioritise their own wishes to the point where a child who is autistic, say, is dragged around to visit any number of people in a few days, so that there is little or no familiarity, or possibility of the routine that is so badly needed. A family that regularly removes a deaf child's hearing aids when the child comes home from school on the grounds that they ought to make the effort to communicate with the family on the family's terms, is guilty of abusive practice.

Since one could go on ad infinitum with examples, the following is a list of many of the assumptions that underlie abusive practice towards disabled children. Fundamentally, abusive practice is based on the attitude that disabled children don't matter as much as non-disabled children. Also:

1. That all disabled children will be better, or feel better if they can be made to appear or behave more like 'normal' children.
2. That disabled children are too used to examination and handling of their bodies to feel embarrassment.
3. That children with severe or complex impairments especially, don't experience the same emotions as non-disabled children.
4. That children with severe impairments can't be consulted.
5. That doctors and others in the medical field always know best.
6. That disabled children need to be taught to understand and/or ignore intrusive behaviour from the general public, as part of learning to be well adjusted.
7. That parents *must* be burdened by caring for disabled children and that we must focus on the parents' needs in order to get the best for the child, rather than the child's needs first and then the parents'.
8. That impairments account for everything that needs

explaining in a disabled child's life.
9. That our common sense judgements about respectful handling of children don't apply to many disabled children in many situations.
10. That what disabled children can express is as much as they can understand.
11. That physically impaired children must also have learning difficulties.

It is vital, therefore, that the abuses of power such as those described before these definitions are seen by us as abuse and are tackled forcefully, because they often lead seamlessly into abuse as defined in law.

Myths about the abuse of disabled children

At this point, it is important to go through – and dispense with – some of the myths surrounding the abuse of disabled children.

This list of myths is drawn mainly from *Bridging the Gap*, but one myth not mentioned in this study has already been dispatched – the assumption that parents and carers of disabled children are saints.[4] If you are a parent please keep in mind that social workers may hold such a view not only of you, but also of others, such as those parents who put themselves forward for the family support schemes where our children spend hours, days or weekends with another family. They may hold the same view about people working as carers in respite care schemes run by local authorities. These people may, of course, be wonderful, but they are more likely to be ordinary, and there is always the possibility that they could be perpetrators of abuse. This book will not encourage you to treat everyone with suspicion, but it will perhaps encourage you to be a little more cautious and, more importantly, to be able to look at the possibility that someone *could* be an abuser if your suspicions are aroused.

There is perhaps an unstated belief that we'd know if someone was a perpetrator – that somehow people who abuse look or behave differently. In truth, perpetrators of sexual abuse in particular often seem the most charming and popular people. They foster this image because then, should any allegation occur, they know that everyone will either dismiss the allegation out of hand, or leap to their defence. How many cases of abuse would have been dealt with earlier and better if people had been able to countenance that a trusted professional, friend or even family member might be capable of abuse?

Perhaps the most all-pervasive myth, and the one that causes most people to fail to notice or report abuse, is that nobody would stoop so low. Of course, the reality is just the opposite. Society sends out all sorts of messages to perpetrators that disabled children are easy, and easily justified, targets. This myth almost certainly arises out of denial; denial because it is painful enough to contemplate the abuse of any child, let alone one whose impairments make them less able to defend themselves or disclose, and denial because acknowledgement would force society to face up to the part it plays in making disabled children more vulnerable to abuse. In the research I quoted earlier, it was discovered that disabled children were twice as likely to suffer neglect and emotional abuse as non-disabled children, with slightly lower (but still disturbingly high) rates for physical and sexual abuse. However, we also have to put into the equation the fact that abuse is four times more likely in institutions than at home.[5] We don't know how the four times and two times go together. We don't know whether in effect disabled children spending time in institutions (which of course they are far more likely to do, whether it's hospital, respite care or residential school) are six times more likely to be abused, eight times, or some other figure. Perhaps it is enough to know that, given approximately a one in eight figure for the non-disabled population (an estimate made by organisations such as the NSPCC), we must be looking at a very large proportion of children being abused in some way. One way or another, this is truly alarming but I have to say it confirms my suspicions having listened to so many disabled people down the years.

Another myth is that abuse doesn't affect disabled children as badly as non-disabled children. This one is unlikely to be believed by parents, but is often believed by professionals who really want to walk away from the whole thing. I find it helpful to point out that the less information or understanding we have about something stressful, the *more* upsetting it becomes. Some would like to believe that a child with learning difficulties won't be so distressed by abuse because they don't really understand. This becomes obvious nonsense when we think about times that we have been to the doctor with disturbing symptoms which they have been unable to diagnose. Our stress levels go through the roof. Yet somehow, if we can name our problem, grave as it may be, it becomes that much easier to cope with.

A fourth fallacy is that disabled children are more likely to make false allegations. Actually, the more dependent a person is, the less likely they are to make even small complaints (think of your own experiences of illness) because they are so aware of their vulnerability to reprisal. The real truth is that disabled children are even less likely to disclose abuse, being all too aware of how easy it would be to punish them for 'making trouble'. One disabled woman told me about some of the abuse she suffered in a residential setting, and added 'You wouldn't *dream* of telling anyone, because you knew how easy it was for the staff to get back at you.'

Another myth which parents and carers are less likely to believe, is that if it has happened, it's best to leave well alone. This is based on the stereotype of disabled children as fragile creatures, by nature emotionally weak. Even Child Protection investigators can fall for this one. I was once involved as a consultant in a case where a disabled girl of 16 had alleged sexual abuse by her father and uncle. The policeman and social worker involved decided not to take her to the proper interview suite on the grounds that this might be too emotionally difficult for her (although all non-disabled youngsters would be taken there). This girl had actually managed to indicate that something was very wrong by determinedly clinging to staff at school and not letting go. This behaviour had brought her to the brink of exclusion. She was damaged, maybe, but definitely not so fragile!

There is also a myth prevalent in the world of professionals. This one says it's impossible for abuse to occur where there has been a lot of professional input. This was repeated only recently to a colleague of mine and is frankly astonishing. It is a simple matter of statistics: the more people there are with access to a child, the greater the chance of one of them being a perpetrator. The underlying assumption, which *no one* in the child protection world should hold, is that all professionals are safe. Most are. Some are not.

Finally there is the myth that says it's impossible to protect disabled children – this is just burying one's head in the sand. Of course it is impossible to protect any child 100 per cent. But all of us could do a great deal more to protect our children than we do now. And that, after all, is what this book is all about.

What is a protective parent of disabled children?

In a way it is hard to use these words together, because one of the most common accusations levelled at parents of disabled children is that they are 'over-protective'. That seems to me an unfortunate phrase, since this behaviour is certainly nothing to do with the kind of protection discussed here. Indeed, whilst it may not constitute abuse, 'over-protection' amounts to abusive practice since it prevents the disabled child from having many normal experiences and, therefore, from developing fully. It may be based partly on a wholly understandable fear about how others may treat the child, but in truth it arises more from an inability to see the child as a real and whole being, who deserves to savour life to the full. The over-protected child is never allowed to take risks and is rarely unsupervised. This is bad news for a child because, whatever their limitations, they have the capacity for winning friends on their own terms. No unsupervised contact really means no friends, yet friends are our birthright. How often have disabled teenagers complained to me about not being allowed to choose their own clothes, let alone go to the shops without their parents. How often have they complained that although they physically could use public transport, their parents won't let them learn to do so alone. The fewer friends a child has, the fewer normal life experiences, the less street-wise they are, and the more vulnerable to abuse because their life is unlike anyone else's.

In a nutshell, Gerrilyn Smith conceives of protective parenthood as a series of concentric circles, with the child at the centre and the protective parent as the closest circle surrounding the child.[6] After that come others that they encounter regularly, and the idea is to try to ensure that the people closest to the child are the protective ones, so that any potential or actual perpetrators of abuse are pushed to the edges of the child's life.

So a protective, as opposed to over-protective carer of any child is one who is deeply interested in the children in their charge; who deliberately builds the children's self-esteem at every opportunity; who listens to their children at least as much as they talk to them; and who stays informed about the other people and other circumstances in the children's lives. The protective adult's behaviour forms a kind of shield around the child – not a shield that keeps out other friendly and loving people, or exciting experiences, but a shield that says to the child 'You are deeply important to me. I think you are wonderful, exactly as you are, and I care that you should always be treated right. I want to hear what makes you happy, but I also want to hear what makes you sad. If something bad is happening to you I shall do my best to ensure that it stops quickly and never happens again.' Never mind that the child might not understand the words, they will certainly pick up the meaning. Even severely brain-damaged children sense people with whom they are safe, relaxing with them, and responding to people who are unknown or unsafe, with tension and tears.

We can't tell our children that we will make sure nothing bad ever happens to them – it's not possible and we would only leave them with a bitter feeling of betrayal when anything went wrong. And let's face it, even we can't behave well all the time. For a thousand reasons we might treat our children in a way that we later regret. Children forgive us more than we could ever hope, but how much more so when we do our best to address the reasons we have mistreated them so that it doesn't get repeated endlessly. My own children have known for some time that when I'm tired I'm bad-tempered and I shout at them, and they have come to accept that as part of who I am. They don't know that I'm doing everything I can to prevent this level of tiredness, but hopefully they'll reap the benefit anyway.

About this book

This book is divided up into three sections. The first section deals with the immediate issues involved when our children are in our own care.

Parents of disabled children have to face the extremely uncomfortable fact that perpetrators of sexual abuse in particular (though not exclusively), are coldly calculating about seeking out jobs and circumstances which maximise not only their access to children they can easily control, but also families that are vulnerable because they are in need of external support. It is one of the most disturbing aspects of child abuse, yet what we have learnt from people convicted of these crimes is also of great help in protecting our children.

Perhaps the single most important consequence of this knowledge lies in the area of building our children's self-esteem. The phrase 'easy to control' has several meanings, but one meaning is children who feel so unloved and bad about themselves that they can be groomed for abuse by demonstrations of affection. The perpetrator then becomes as needed as they are feared, and the child is both easily confused about their real intentions and, more seriously, too scared of the loss of the apparent affection to disclose to others what is happening. For this reason, throughout the book you will find references to ways of helping your children to feel loved and good about themselves, but Chapter One deals specifically with building your child's self-image.

Another meaning of 'easy to control' lies in the area of preventing the child from telling. A child who is successfully using *any* system of communication, verbal or otherwise, with their parents or carers, is much less of a target than one who has little or no communication with those people. I want to emphasise that I am including amongst children who can successfully communicate those who have only Yes or No signals, but with whom parents and carers communicate a great deal. Even those children who have only involuntary communication but whose parents and carers take a lot of notice of those signals, are safer than children who have speech but are never listened to, only talked at. So Chapter Two looks in detail at how we can maximise our communication with disabled children, to keep them safer. It does not take any great insight to understand why the need for intimate care (toileting, bathing, dressing and so on) is a risk factor. In fact it presents us with many challenges if we want to keep our children safe. Equally, it is easy to see that our children need much more help to develop positive sexual identities and healthy attitudes towards sexuality, so I examine these two areas in Chapters Three and Four.

The second section of the book looks at matters arising when our children are in the care of others. One of the difficulties faced by parents of disabled children is the number of other people (over and above those encountered by non-disabled children) who certainly start out as strangers, and who enter our children's lives. So there are drivers and escorts, support teachers, home care workers and health visitors, and any number of doctors and therapists. Chapter Five examines the issues involved.

Another aspect of our children's contact with the medical establishment is the issue of medical intervention. Parents (particularly those who are non-disabled) are very vulnerable to professionals – especially doctors – who promise to do things to make our children 'more normal'. In the name of this mythical notion our children may find their lives to be just one series of hospital appointments and stays after another. Chapter Six will help parents think through the pros and cons of medical intervention and the impact it may have on the child's overall development and self-esteem.

Schooling can also be a completely different experience for some disabled children to that of others, and even when they are in mainstream schools, there are obstacles to be faced which parents need to be alert to in order to help their children deal successfully with them. Chapter Seven helps to pinpoint possible problems, with ideas to assist parents in finding out information that will help in assessing just how safe the school may be.

The focus of this book is on the prevention of abuse. However, it is also vital that we are able to recognise signs of abuse and are equipped to deal with the consequences. The last section of the book helps us to know how to recognise and deal with abuse. It is extraordinary that we know that disabled children are abused in great numbers, yet they are rarely the subject of Child Protection referrals. One reason is because people overlook signs and indicators that would certainly alert them were the child non-disabled. Chapter Eight looks at signs and indicators of abuse in disabled children, the extent to which they are the same and also how they vary from those in non-disabled children. The final chapter gives advice on dealing with the situation when abuse has occurred, and reassures us, perhaps, that all is not lost.

Section One
Our Children in our Care

Chapter One

Self-Image

Self-image, or how we see ourselves, and how we feel about ourselves deep down, is absolutely critical to our ability to function well in the world. When we feel good about ourselves we are likely to do well, or at least to do our best. When we feel bad about ourselves we may be unable to do anything at all. Or perhaps we mess up what we try to do. Our level of self-esteem is made apparent by things like our respect for our own bodies and the force with which we will demand that our physical and emotional needs be met. It shows in how emotionally resilient we are – or are not. It is particularly relevant to the subject of this book that people with high self-esteem refuse to accept maltreatment or neglect.

I once read a book by a South African woman who had been imprisoned by the apartheid regime.[1] For some reason, the most potent moment for me was where she described her refusal to accept food that had been placed on the cell floor. (Her door would be opened and the food placed on the floor, rather than passed to her.) She was proud enough of herself to refuse to eat it like this. She pointed out that she was not a dog, and finally went on hunger strike until they agreed to hand her her food in a more dignified way.

Many of us are familiar with the fact that our self-image is complicated, and changes. It is complex in as much as our identities are complex and the messages we receive about those identities vary according to the situations we are in or the people surrounding us. I am disabled, and a woman, a mother and a professional; I'm also Jewish, middle-class, white, English, middle-aged and heterosexual. I have acquired bits of positive and negative self-image attached to all of these, and what surfaces often depends on the company and circumstances I find myself in. But ultimately there is a core identity, a feeling of me-ness on which all the others rest. It is this that I fall back on when I'm up against it and which either boosts me or lets me down.

So in some situations we can sparkle. We feel respected and loved and we show ourselves at our best. In others we feel people neither respect us nor expect much of us and then it is *only* our deep internal self-respect which can carry us through. With enough self-respect we can prove to others that they underestimated us. Without it, we tend to sink and low expectations become self-prophesying. Also, when we feel good about ourselves we demand to be treated well. When we feel bad about ourselves we are more inclined to feel we just have to accept anything that comes our way. So our self-image, in all its layers, is really important in our ability to stick up for our rights and to do well.

Self-image is derived from many different sources. Of course it begins with the child internalising what their parents or carers communicate to them about how good, clever, strong, pretty/handsome and loveable they are.

But then there are also many external influences which parents cannot control, but can deal with if they are recognised. Obviously the attitudes of the people, especially the other family members and children, with whom the child mixes are very important. So too, however, are media images, in books, videos and films, TV and advertisements. The language we use also says a lot about our attitudes towards certain groups within society and the child will absorb these messages.

Language, disability and self-image

The first time I understood the role that language had played in my own self-image was when I realised how often my leg was described as a *bad* leg.[2] Then I realised people asked 'What's *wrong* with your leg?' (I was very happy recently when a child at nursery asked me that question. Almost in unison my girls said 'There's nothing *wrong* with it, it's just short'.) When you think about it there is always a more accurate and informative word than bad, which is a value judgement. So you might say 'He has a painful back' or 'She has a weak eye.' It is better to say something like 'She has a short fuse' than 'She has a bad temper.'

It also has to be remembered that people don't confine themselves to describing bits of us as bad. Recently I visited a young disabled woman in a hostel. It was tea-time, and I was waiting for transport to leave, when one young woman choked on her food. Her helper rushed to condemn her, rather than taking any responsibility, saying 'Ooh, she is bad. She won't concentrate.' Even if people don't condemn our whole beings overtly like that, if we hear ourselves described as having bad body parts or bad functioning often enough, we begin to internalise that message. So we may either feel that our leg/arm/eye is bad, or come to believe that we are bad altogether.

When it formed, one of the first things the disability movement addressed, was language. We rejected a number of terms (like 'cripples', 'handicapped', and '*the* disabled') and at the time opted for 'people with disabilities', because we felt that it was important to stress that we were first and foremost human beings. But as time went on and we explored the roots of our mistreatment in society (our oppression), the movement opted for 'disabled people', stressing that we are not the ones with a problem; society gives us problems, dis-ables us, by setting up barriers to our participation.

However, these linguistic decisions are subject to change, and if you are on the outside looking in, this can be frustrating and difficult. But if you are prepared to listen to the reasons for these changes, you will not only learn a great deal but also be able to give your child a sound start. One problem many parents and professionals have is of being unaware of exactly who is generating 'politically correct' language. Workers often find their employers requiring them to use phrases like 'special needs' only to find disabled people rejecting these absolutely. The point is that this and many other phrases have been coined by non-disabled people, often health and education professionals, without consulting the disability movement. Surely any group within society has a right to define itself. So I always accept the self-generated terms put forward by any section of the community, in preference to ones I have picked up elsewhere. But we will make mistakes and we do have to be prepared for constant learning, and ultimately, when we are speaking to any particular individual, we have to honour the language they desire.

The area of general terms, then, can be fairly tricky. But there are some rules that we can stick to very easily. These deal with what we should *not* call children.

- We should not call them by their conditions. (*He is a* CP; *she is an epileptic, he is an* MLD *[mild learning difficulties].*)
- We should not call children by the causes of their impairments. (*She is an* RTA *[road traffic accident]; he is a polio; she is a C4 [spinal injury at the level of the fourth cervical vertebra].*)
- We should not label children by the equipment they use. (*He is a manual [the type of wheelchair], she is a catheter; he's a Bliss board.*)
- We should not call children by the procedures they need for daily life. (*She is a tube [i.e. tube fed]; he's a toileter.*)
- We should not call children by the source of funding for the service they receive. (*He's a Section 11; she's an* HA *[health authority funded]; he's a private.*)

This language is extremely common and utterly dehumanising. We can't possibly expect children to have self-respect and high self-esteem if they hear themselves described in these ways. (It has to be said that disabled adults are just as vulnerable to the effect of these terms. I have had adults introduce themselves to me thus: 'Hello, I'm a C6' or 'Hello, I'm a CP'.) For this reason such language is pilloried in the disability movement's jokes. For example:

Waiter: We don't allow wheelchairs in here.
Punter: It's not my wheelchair that's hungry.

Again parents do have a responsibility for challenging the use of such language, however uncomfortable that is. Sure enough you may get a hostile response, but stick to your guns! If necessary refer the offending person(s) to the Chailey Heritage Charter of Children's Rights which demands that children be called by their names at all times (see Resources section). Disabled parents are usually at an advantage because they have already had a lifetime of having to challenge such language. Those who never plucked up the courage on their own behalf may find themselves unexpectedly brave in defence of their children!

Disability images

So children may have a poor self-image for reasons that have nothing to do with the quality of our parenting. Many people have noted how quickly racism affects children, for instance, so that by the time they are four or five, black children can develop feelings of inferiority and dirtiness, regardless of the efforts their parents and families have made to model pride in being black.[3] Nevertheless parents who communicate pride in the child for all they are (*not*, in the case of disabled children, *despite* their disability) provide an important safeguard against the worst effects of prejudice and discrimination by others.

Non-disabled parents are rarely aware of the images of disability that are actually prevalent and deeply affect disabled children, just because in their own lives there have been no guidelines towards recognising these damaging representations. David Hevey's book, *The Creatures That Time Forgot*, goes into disability imagery in detail.[4]

Disability as badness

The most powerful and perhaps deep-seated image, originating centuries ago, but perpetuated by children's and adult fiction, is that of the disabled person as being intrinsically bad. Disability is commonly used as a metaphor for evil; in other words, we are expected to recognise the baddy as such, simply because they are disabled in some way, before their wrong-doing has been pointed out. We instantly recognise the wicked witch from her gnarled, arthritic hands and her deformed spine (or hunchback, as the books would describe it), and know that the pirate with one hand or one eye or a wooden leg is likely to be the bad guy in the story. I have trained thousands of people in disability equality and after showing them these familiar images I always ask, 'How many of you said to yourselves that that's a disabled woman or man?' Out of these thousands of people only one woman has ever said that she had made that connection. Everyone else has been shocked to realise that they have always had the equation of disability with evil planted in their minds at a subconscious level.

These images of disability as a sign of evil started when spiritual and religious leaders around the world explained it as punishment for wrong-doing. Although there are few today in Europe who consciously hold this belief, the media images ensure its presence at the back of our minds and it emerges clearly in comments like 'What a shame' when someone sees a disabled person. These days we may not think we mean 'what a thing to be ashamed of', but that is certainly where the expression derives from. All this explains perfectly the terms discussed earlier. It is of great interest that the use of 'bad' in relation to disability is common in many languages, including non-Western ones, and is also used in relation to health. Thus doctors are there to stop you feeling 'bad' and to help you feel 'better'. In French the word for ill is the same as the word for bad.

I do not mean to suggest that religion is simply bad news for disabled people. But it is clear that often even those who have a strong faith have a battle with ancient and condemnatory ideas. Michael Hull, who is blind, takes us through this in his book *Touching the Rock*.[5] He is a deeply religious Christian and recalls the time when a church member told him that God had said He could cure Hull through this man. The latter then turned up at Hull's house and told him he was blind because he didn't have enough faith. When Hull illustrated how deep his faith was his visitor tried a parallel tack, claiming it was because he didn't read his Bible enough. Hull explained patiently that he read his Bible in Braille every day for at least twenty minutes and that there were a lot of people out there who never read it but had perfect sight!

The message for parents and carers then is that, whatever our faith or lack of it, we need to be aware of the interpretations and representations that will be damaging to our child's self-image and we should try to help arm our child against that.

Evil images lead to disabled children feeling that they are intrinsically bad; they lead to lowered self-esteem and often a desperation to prove that they are good. This behaviour makes them very vulnerable to manipulation by others who can get the child to do what they want by giving or withholding approval. If parents are failing to give enough approval, a perpetrator can move in and gain the child's trust by offering it. Some children, on the other hand, react by behaving abominably, with the implied message 'If you think I'm bad I'll show you what bad is!'. Again a perpetrator can move in on such a child by making out they are the only ones who think this child is good.

Obviously, if the problem of feeling bad is coming only from the implied social disapproval of harmful images, a parent can feel both bewildered and annoyed at the child's desperation for approval or, alternatively, awful behaviour. Sometimes it helps to make it explicit that the child is not and never has been bad, but it is also very helpful to address the childhood images that children are exposed to directly. For instance, since we can't prevent children encountering the wicked witch, we can at least point out that we disapprove of using gender, age or impairment in this way. We can point out that women like her in terms of her physical qualities can also be kind, helpful and loving.

An equivalent of the evil image in relation to people with learning difficulties is that of the evil zombie – a person with no brain at all who simply destroys everything in sight. This is almost entirely confined to adult fiction. It certainly accounts for some of the fear the public exhibit around people with learning difficulties, but does not get transmitted directly to children. Instead, the primary image for youngsters is that of the village idiot; Simple Simon from the nursery rhyme, for example. Again, children with learning difficulties don't take long to pick up the sense of shame associated with being a laughing stock.

Invisibility

Statistically speaking, of course, disabled people are barely represented at all in any kind of fiction. In other words, given the high proportion of people with some impairment or other, it is amazing how rarely they feature in any way. This carries its own dangers. The most obvious is that with so few adult role models for disabled children, large numbers of disabled youngsters have believed that when they turn 21 or 18, they will become non-disabled. Many face a traumatic period, usually in their teens, when they finally realise that in fact they will always have their impairments (see Micheline Mason in *Images of Ourselves*).[6] Less obvious perhaps, is the message received by perpetrators: 'These children are out of sight and therefore out of mind. No one will notice or care what happens to them.' Unfortunately, with our children often in institutions far away from our own homes, this has too often been the case.

Many women are aware of how damaging it is that television and films tend only to show young, 'beautiful' white women, and young strong white men with whatever is currently considered to be the perfect kind of body. We know it is problematic for non-disabled women, white and black, who can do all sorts of things to themselves in their efforts to match up to these images. How much more harmful can it be when you are *never* even going to be on the starting block?

The absence of images of disabled people is particularly acute, and therefore particularly dangerous, for black disabled people. They rarely feature in posters, the newspapers, TV or films. I was once running a disability equality course in an inner London borough which has one of the highest proportions of ethnic minority communities anywhere and which includes many war victims. Yet when I raised the issue of black disabled people, one of the participants protested that there were none in that borough! Many have acknowledged how potent media images are, such as the effect on women of film stars and models being so thin they verge on skeletal, but we have yet to fully understand the danger of the absence of whole groups of people from popular imagery.

One important area for children, in which this absence is beginning to be addressed, is that of the availability of appropriate dolls. It is now possible to buy some dolls with 'impairments' and disability equipment (eg crutches and wheelchairs), and it is also easier, though not easy enough, to find black dolls.

Parents and carers may well have little influence, as individuals, on the writers of fiction, for example, but we can complain to public bodies, like schools, voluntary organisations or libraries, if their publicity material fails to represent disabled people, in all their diversity. It really isn't on to allow people to continue to believe that they are representing *all* disabled people with the stale old images of a white chappie in a wheelchair!

Disability as illness

The second most potent image of disabled people, after that of disability as badness, arises out of what the disability movement calls the medical model of disability. This took over from the spiritual or religious model, in explicit, or conscious terms, when and where medics acquired the status and position previously occupied by religious leaders. Essentially it describes disabled people as abnormal and in need of medical attention, a state which we equate with illness. Since ill people are often weak and vulnerable, these traits are then ascribed to disabled people even when they are in the rudest of good health. It turns disabled people into victims, permanently dependent on others for help, in particular medical professionals.

It also sends disabled children the message that they are not *good enough* as they are, since someone must make them *better*. It tells them, and unfortunately their parents, that it is important that something be done to them to make them more 'normal', and acceptable. This can lead to any amount of abusive practice in terms of equipment (like cumbersome artificial arms), exercises and professional intervention which interferes with their everyday lives. For example, within a group of disabled girls that I worked with, each girl had had around eight operations by the time she was a teenager, in the name of the normality of being able to walk. Most of them still use wheelchairs and have had great chunks of their young lives distorted by hospitalisation.

I would never suggest that disabled children should not have any equipment, exercises or operations; that would be a nonsense. But, as I will detail in Chapter Five, it is incumbent on parents and legal guardians to assess carefully the goal behind these interventions, as medical intervention can sometimes be emotionally and physically abusive to the child.

Tragic, brave victims

Victim imagery is perpetuated largely through charity advertising. Disabled people have been particularly offended, for instance, by campaigns such as those by the Multiple Sclerosis Society, depicting 'victims' of the disease as previously beautiful people with strips torn out (eyes, spines, etc.), with the legend 'When this goes everything goes' and, on every poster, 'A Hope in Hell', meaning the society is a hope in the hell of MS. I remember my revulsion on seeing one of these advertisements on my journey to visit a friend who had just been diagnosed as having MS. I kept imagining her seeing it and having to fight with the idea that she was on her way to a living hell. (Incidentally, she has since had a baby and is living a full and rewarding life.)

Newspapers, however, also carry such images. They too love stories of disabled people who were once helpless, but thanks to the tireless work of doctors, nurses and physiotherapists, now walk, or stand by themselves. The favourite words used by newspapers in describing disabled people are 'tragic' and 'brave'. This inspired one singing group of disabled people to call themselves 'The Tragic but Brave Roadshow'.

It is very hard, in the face of this helpless victim imagery, for disabled children to feel there is any chance of being fit, assertive and independent. On the other hand they often feel bludgeoned into being brave, and smile determinedly through the most appalling mistreatment. It is not difficult to see how dangerous all this is for the children, because if they have been taught they must accept pain it becomes difficult, if not impossible, to distinguish between pain that should never have been inflicted and pain that is unavoidable, but transient. As we shall see in Chapter Six, it also carries dangers for the parents.

Facing negative attitudes

In her book *Pride Against Prejudice* (which is a very useful read), Jenny Morris lists some of the most common attitudes that confront disabled people of all ages.[7] Amongst the ones I have not yet picked out are:

- That nothing can be gained from the experience [of disability].
- That disabled people constantly suffer and that any suffering is nasty, unjust, to be feared and retreated from.
- That disabled people can't ever really accept their condition, and if they appear to be leading a full and contented life, or are simply cheerful, they are just 'putting a brave face on it'.
- That disability has affected them psychologically, making them bitter and neurotic.

As I say, this is just a sample. We could add to this list the stereotypes that are applied by large numbers of non-disabled people. A stereotype is like an attitude, but is more vicious because it is often bi-polar (that is, composed of two opposing assumptions) and so the objects of the stereotyping can be caught somewhere in the middle. For black people then, a typical one is 'Blacks are lazy vs working like a black'. It's the last attitude quoted from Jenny Morris that reminded me of this, because one of the most potent stereotypes disabled people have to face from childhood on, is 'You people are always so happy vs bitter and twisted' . This has its roots firmly in the religious model of disability whereby impairment is associated with evil but suffering is 'saintly', but the point is there is no way out of it. Whatever my mood or personality, people can apply one end or the other to me. To say it is confusing to face someone telling you one end one day and the other the next, is a true understatement. It can be no better if, like many people with Down's syndrome in particular, you are permanently faced not only with the 'You people are always so happy' pole, but also with a *demand* to stay that way.

Just the other day I met someone who works in a hostel for adults with learning difficulties. She recalled how a member of staff had, as usual, told one of the residents to 'Cheer up, Tom, smile' and how he had obliged with a fixed and inane grin. When my friend then approached him and said she didn't mind if he wanted to look miserable with her, he was able to be real and began to talk about the recent death of his mother (which, by the way, he had not been allowed to mourn with the rest of the family, having been prevented from attending the funeral).

It is incredibly hard to fight your way free of all this rubbish coming at you day after day, and children do need their parents' permission *not* to be permanently sweet and understanding about it all. Yes, they can be encouraged to be polite up to a point, but if they are required to absorb all these negative attitudes and destructive stereotypes, they can lose sight of who they really are . . . and what's more those people go unchallenged. Perhaps as parents we need to model for our children reacting as the situation and our moods take us, because as parents we also are on the receiving end of much of this. If our children witness us sometimes being patient and polite, sometimes blanking people, sometimes coming out with a razor sharp and funny (to us) comment, and sometimes being downright rude or angry, it will help them enormously.

This is especially true in relation to the stereotype around sexuality. This suggests that 'Disabled people have no sexuality vs they are all sex-mad monsters'. It is true that the first pole is more likely to be applied to people with visible, physical impairments and the second to people with learning difficulties, but not exclusively so. This will be dealt with at greater length in Chapter Four.

Helping children achieve a positive self-image

In the first place, we have to be aware of what our children are contending with. When we are on the lookout for the images entering their world, then and only then, can we give them tools to deal with such imagery.

Whilst we cannot prevent our children from seeing videos, or reading books containing the wicked witch or the evil pirate, *we can point out to them that it is wrong that people should have used impairments to represent badness*. It is no different to my having to point out to my girls that it is wrong that so many of the bad people in Disney films are women, when in real life men do most of the grand-scale bad things. If I actually tried to stop them watching these videos that all their friends have, *I* would be the wicked witch! But they do listen to my attempts to analyse the images.

We may also need to talk to staff in our children's schools. Not that long ago I walked into the foyer of a 'special' school to be met by an enormous picture of a one-eyed and one-legged pirate. As I was running a course for the staff I had a perfect opportunity to raise the issue of the display and the staff were genuinely mortified that it had not occurred to them (being non-disabled), that they were perpetuating damaging ideas for the children in their care. We can also talk to others charged with the care of our children and ask them to be sure to counteract any negative images our children might encounter whilst with them.

We can help our children, too, in a way that can be immensely enjoyable for us. That is by having a celebratory attitude to the equipment that must be used, rather than one which says 'Oh well, we just have to put up with this ugly chair' or whatever they use. I remember a beautiful walking stick that Ken and Jean Westmacott, who I mention later, helped a student make for a child in Africa. It was made of wood, good and sturdy with a ferrel at the base, but wiggly and painted to look like a bright snake! I recall, too, my young deaf friend who got so sick of people wanting her to hide her hearing aids beneath her hair that she had them painted bright colours. And it's not unusual to see quite a few youngsters parading in gaudily decorated wheelchairs. I strongly believe that the more youngsters can make their equipment their own in this way, and shout to the world 'I enjoy who I am', the more they will attract the attention of mentally healthy people and the less they will attract perpetrators of abuse.

Another critical thing we can do is to make absolutely sure that our disabled children are included in family photos and home videos. So many disabled adults have complained about being excluded from these as children that it is an issue that has been actively explored.[8] Blind children would benefit from audio tapes of all the family talking, including themselves. One reason for doing this is so that they *do* identify themselves as a family member – it is even more critical if they go to a residential boarding school. It also helps them to see and hear themselves as others do, and so contributes to them building a realistic perception of themselves. Some parents obviously think this is cruel; but that in itself suggests that their own perception of their child is very negatively tainted. I believe it is not cruel, but helps the child in any number of ways.

I remember the first time I saw myself walking on a caliper. It was quite mind-blowing because one's brain adjusts to the rock and roll of such a gait, and it is easy to forget that one's movement is indeed abnormal. At the time, two main thoughts struck me. The first was 'Well, no wonder people stop for a second look, or even stare' not negatively, but just as a matter of fact. The second was an increased acknowledgement of how much hard work walking was for me, so that in fact seeing myself served to *increase* my self-respect, not decrease it. We must not patronise disabled children by imagining that they can't cope with their own reality. If those around them are respectful and matter-of-fact, they will probably be able to feel self-respect too, though it is possible that some things (which for instance they can't see just by looking at themselves or looking in a mirror) might be upsetting. Again, the most respectful approach is to assume that they will be able to get past the upset, once they have been allowed to express it. Surely it's true that all of us at some time in our lives get an unpleasant surprise when someone holds a mirror up to us – whether it is something to do with our manner, our laughter, or another aspect of ourselves. If a friend does it in a supportive way it is useful, not damaging.

If our child is at a stage where playing with dolls is enjoyable, then we can look out for disabled dolls. They don't have to have the same impairment or equipment as our child; what is important is simply that they are amongst the playthings. And we can give them as presents to non-disabled children too – especially those who may be friends with our children. This helps them to accept impairment as a part of their normality, not as something separate from it.

In building up our child's self-esteem, it is enormously helpful if they have contact with disabled adults, particularly, but not exclusively, those who share the same impairment. Having positive role models of adults leading successful lives, *with* their impairments and *despite* the oppression, is incredibly positive. For example, staff in one institution were very concerned that they had been unable to help one boy who was a wheelchair user to shift the invisible, but non-disabled, boy he 'kept' under his bed. This lad, unlike himself, could run around and play football. Nothing they could say or do had made any difference. Finally they appealed to a very positive disabled man, who admittedly had counselling skills, to come and talk to the boy. This man achieved in half an hour what the non-disabled staff had been unable to achieve in months. He simply asked of the boy, from his own wheelchair, 'What's so great about walking?' He talked a little about the sports he played, listened a little and that was that. But this does not have to happen on an individual basis. It could be arranged through local disability organisations and schools, or groups of parents, and can develop according to the groups' demands and the skills of the disabled adults.

Performance can be inspiring too, and there are groups of disabled people who take performance to disabled young people. For instance, Graeae Theatre Company, Strathcona, Heart 'n' Soul, and Amici Dance company do this, but we can contact disability arts organisations, find out what's happening and take our children to shows and events. There are disability arts organisations in many regions of the country, covering many types of art, and addressed to many types of people. We can find out about local disability arts organisations from any local information centre, not necessarily one specialising in disability information.

But as parents and carers we can also make a tremendous difference by remembering to give praise whenever it is due. With disabled children praise for effort, and praise for each small step on the way to a big achievement, is even more important than for non-disabled children. It is critical, too, to set appropriate goals and not wait till a child can do what their non-disabled brothers and sisters can do. Since a disabled child's developmental landmarks may be different, we must make sure they have something practical to aim for and that their achievements are indeed marked. If, for example, our child is never going to walk, they will miss out on the natural delight of adults when infants toddle for the first time. So we will need to look out for other skills and mark them with delight and approval. Another way of helping a child feel that they are achieving is simply to mark their passage through the years in imaginative ways. For instance, we could have one wall of a room which we could paint a different colour to mark each passing quarter of a year, or a mural that would have a detail added to mark the acquisition of each new skill, however small.

There are other less obvious ways of helping your child develop an appropriate sense of self-esteem. It is critical that parents lay down the same rules for their disabled as their non-disabled children. A child who feels they can do whatever they like is just as likely to feel uncared for as a child whose parents are too strict. Far too many parents, carers and professionals have been guilty of failing to lay down the same rules for their disabled youngsters as they do for non-disabled youngsters. This is dangerous in several ways. In the first place it causes great resentment amongst brothers and sisters, who are often already suffering a lack of attention in comparison to their disabled sibling. Secondly, it can give a disabled child a completely artificial sense of power, which is usually expressed in ways that make other youngsters, and indeed adults, want to avoid them. So their self-image may be that of someone who can do whatever they like, but in reality, their options will diminish as fewer and fewer people want to spend time with them. As I mentioned earlier, this can leave the disabled child isolated and therefore vulnerable to perpetrators of abuse. Thirdly it can add a dangerous layer of confusion if there are signs and indicators of abuse. Thus if a teenager has never been told when and where it is appropriate to masturbate – and when it is not – masturbating in public could cause concern as a possible indicator of sexual abuse. If there are other signs, disentangling it all becomes very difficult. Or investigators could dismiss the concern on the grounds that the young person simply does not understand social norms.

It may sometimes take more ingenuity to teach disabled children social rules, but it is extremely important that we do so. It allows a child to develop a self-image that includes knowing how to behave, something in which they can take a genuine pride and for which they will receive approval and acceptance.

In order for a child to develop a positive self-image, we particularly need to encourage and show approval of assertiveness, even though assertive children can challenge our own authority! Assertiveness is really about a person's ability to hold their own, knowing what they want and being able to keep their eye on that, veering from it only through negotiation, not force. However, we need to be clear about the difference between assertiveness and selfishness. If, in trying to assist our children, we only encourage them to satisfy their own needs and wishes at the expense of others, they will be assertive – but extremely unpopular! Equally, assertiveness is not the same as aggression. My colleague, Saadlia Neilson and I adapted a couple of charters of assertive rights, with disabled children in focus. (See Appendix I for details). We hope that this might be the starting point for the development of a national charter of disabled children's rights.

Finally, it is important that we understand what the disability movement calls the social model of disability and keep working out what it means in practical terms for the whole family. Essentially, it states that rather than disability being about badness or helplessness and abnormality, or dependence on charity, it is a socially constructed process whereby disabled people are prevented from taking their full place in society by barriers erected by non-disabled people. These barriers may be attitudes, but are also physical (lack of lifts, for example) structural (such as lack of Brailled, taped or signed information), or institutional (such as the failure to recruit disabled staff). Hence the joke in the movement: 'What's your disability then?' 'Your steps, mate.'

Understanding this model of disability, and pushing for disabled people's full inclusion in society, is extremely empowering for parents, carers and disabled children alike, despite the magnitude of the battles that often face us. This is because other approaches keep the spotlight on the disabled individual, suggesting that they are the problem, or they have the problem. Thus they are the ones expected to change, adjust, get better. With the social model, suddenly the blame is firmly placed outside, on society as a whole, and disabled people are getting the message that they are fine as they are. In child protection terms this is of enormous importance, because then perpetrators cannot convince a disabled child to accept abuse on the grounds of it making them more acceptable or normal.

I conclude this chapter with extracts from a letter to the *Guardian* newspaper (8/10/96) from Richard M Thompson in response to an article about prenatal screening to prevent the births of babies with impairments:

For the four and a half years of her brief life I was proud to be the father of a beautiful but massively handicapped little girl. She was blind, incontinent, incapable of speech or verbal comprehension, and totally dependent on others. She never knew my name, but came to know my grip, my touch and my voice and loved me as she never loved another . . . It was not her handicaps which created Hell in my life. All she created was love and joy. It was the society we lived in which handicapped us . . . Her pain could be moderated through medicine, and her life and joy were a fluttering, incandescent flame that brightened and warmed the lives of many others . . .

Chapter Two

Communicating with our Children

I must start this chapter with a statement of my own philosophy about communication with disabled children. This is that I hold that there is no such thing as a non-communicating child. The instant we maintain such a belief about any particular child, it is tantamount to abandoning any meaningful relationship with them – indeed it is abandoning them. Certainly some of our children can only communicate unintentionally; that is, we have to interpret body language, facial expressions and behaviours like crying and make the best guesses we can (which increasingly become informed guesses), about what the child is feeling or wanting. Nevertheless, since this is the *giving and receiving* of signals, it *is* communication, and can be vital in working out what the child may be experiencing.

Good communication – or at least the best we can achieve with each individual child – is a large and vital part of the patchwork of protective cloak we need to place around them. It sends out messages to the child and to others about how much we value them, and gives the child the best possible chance of telling or showing us when things are going wrong. It also maximises our chances of picking these things up. This, of course, is true for every parent and carer, not just those whose children are disabled.

I'd like to illustrate my philosophy with a couple of examples from my time in Kenya. On one return visit a friend took me to a project for disabled children. As we went around, one member of staff pointed to a boy and said, 'He's a non-communicating child.' But at that moment, this lad was standing gazing into the distance and rocking from one foot to the other going 'AaaAAaa, aaaAAaa' over and over. I decided to experiment and stood some six feet away and imitated this sound. His head shot round fast as he looked to see where else *his* sound could possibly have come from. That meant he had hearing, could recognise his sound when it came from elsewhere and that he was interested. That showed me that there were openings that could be explored towards developing communication with him.

Then, at the polio clinic where I worked there was a little boy I will call Mwangi. Sometimes he talked, sometimes he withdrew utterly inside himself and simply fluttered his hands in front of his face. It seemed to me to be worth trying to get through, rather than waiting for him to 'come out' again. Sometimes it was enough just to put my face close to his, smile, and say 'Mwangi, hello' a few times. Sometimes it took more ingenuity. I would play at crying, explaining to the other, gobsmacked children, that I was crying because he wouldn't talk to me. This worked nearly every time, eventually producing a smile and a giggle. If all that failed I would pick him up and cuddle him, put my nose on his nose, say his name lots and talk to him and finally he would re-emerge from his inner world. I am not suggesting we should never let children enter or stay for a while in these inner worlds; they obviously go there for safety. The point is that we don't have to imagine they *must* be lost to us once they do that; that there is no way to communicate to them that they are safe now. The challenge is *how* to communicate that they are safe; a fascinating challenge. But we must also be prepared to stop if the child can't emerge. They would if they could.

Some of our children may be able to give us only yes/no signals intentionally; they may understand very little, or absolutely everything. Some of our children will be able to understand much more than they can say, others will be able to say much more than they can actually understand. Some will have great difficulty formulating their thoughts, others will have difficulty formulating their words. Some will be able to pay attention for long periods, others for short periods only. Some will have little or no hearing. Some will have no physical impairment, but a specific language disorder. My discussion is inclusive of every single child, without exception. When I use the words 'listen to' or 'talk to' I intend them to imply the use of *any* communication system, verbal or non verbal, formal or informal. So your listening may be observing your child's body language; it may be paying attention to icons on an electronic communication board; it may be watching signs.

If love is the foundation of relationships with our children, then communication is the cement. The more we communicate the more we understand each other and the greater the trust between us. There is no doubt that the more the lines of communication are open with our children, the more protected they will be, for several important reasons.

First, when we bother to listen or attend to our children they feel valued. Also we are giving them the message that what they have to say is important enough for us to spend time on. When children can take for granted our attention to what they want to tell us (most of the time) they may let us know the very smallest things that are bothering them, often unaware of the significance of the message. They are also more likely to feel that they can let us know about much worse things. Sometimes we can reassure them about things they thought were terrible; on other occasions they may tell us something they thought was not a big deal, but which we view as very serious. Sometimes the things they let us know are the first indications that abuse or abusive practice might have occurred (see Chapter Eight).

As well as building our child's self-esteem, listening to them, and taking in what they say, ensures we get the most information about their world. For instance, I was mystified at first when one of my daughters pointed to a chair at nursery school and told me it was naughty. But by listening to their play I worked out that their teacher employs the old-fashioned punishment of sitting children on the 'naughty chair' when they are unruly. (Personally I dislike this intensely, but that is not the point.)

Everyday non-verbal communication

So it is critical that we all learn to 'read' our children (ie notice how they express themselves, what their body language can tell us, what their behaviour signifies) as best we can. This is important for all children, whether or not they are capable of speech, because, of course, children tell us far more through play and behaviour than they do through speech often right up to adulthood. What can happen, though, is that once children are old enough to be expected to talk, we forget about the wide range of skills we have in communicating without words. We can forget how much we understood our babies, often long before they even reached the babbling stage!

One way I find incredibly helpful in communicating with children who are either pre-verbal, or using non-verbal communication, is to imitate the sounds, movements or facial expressions they make. Children adore this because it puts the power in their hands. They don't *have* to attend to you, but it tells them you are paying attention to them and placing some importance on their communication. I usually find that if I echo a sound or movement exactly, the child laughs and repeats it several times. Then they start to experiment with new ones, to see if I can copy those too. This game can go on as long as it holds the child's interest, or for as long as I can give, but it is immensely enjoyable and both of you can learn a great deal from it. So it serves two main purposes: it tells the child their communication is important and it stimulates them to experiment.

Even when children are verbal, this remains a powerful tool. Sometimes, when we don't understand what a child has said, if we repeat it with a little question mark in our voices, they will expand on it to help us out. If we think they are having us on, repetition with a raised eyebrow, perhaps, prompts them to say, 'No, not really.' Sometimes it just gives us breathing space to consider our response. Either way, children become used to the idea that their communication will get a response, not vanish into thin air, and this is critical to their sense of being able to gain protection when things go wrong.

We are more skilled than we think

We can also usefully remind ourselves of the communication skills we use with each other on a daily basis. All of us are inclined to use noises – perhaps the click of the tongue to indicate disapproval, or the 'Uh-oh' that says we have spotted a problem. Our children might understand these and they might use noises we can understand. We use smell, colour, jewellery, clothes and hairstyles to communicate.

We do these things unconsciously some of the time and very deliberately at others. For instance, we may not think twice about what clothes we throw on to slop around in at the weekend, whereas if we are going to meet a new date, we put a lot of thought into choosing something that will show us at our best. Even when we are doing these things unconsciously, it *is* communicating (our colour choices reflect our personalities and moods, for instance), and therefore all of them can be changed deliberately to see whether they are noticed by a child and how the child reacts to them. We hum and sing, often communicating our emotions without meaning to. We touch, stroke, cuddle, squeeze and tickle. We laugh, cry, yell and yawn; all of which communicate. We look, look away. We participate and withdraw. We play. True enough, how all these are interpreted will vary with age, culture, gender, role, experience and so on, and we had better be sure that interpretations match the intentions. A classic paradox is that while white Westerners consider it rude of a child to look away when they are being told off, many other cultures consider it rude for the child to make eye contact with the adult. But communicate we can and interpret we do, so in fact we have many options at our disposal which we can use and adapt for any particular child.

Touch, in all its variety, can be especially important, since many children can notice and interpret different kinds of touch more easily than variations in other types of communication. Also touch is more important to children with certain impairments – blindness is the obvious one, but it can be very helpful with autistic children, too, especially allowing them to touch you. I remember one little girl who was autistic who used to approach me and feel the caliper that I wore at the time to check it was me and to acknowledge that I had arrived. It was clear that touch was her main source of information about the world; I also remember seeing her in the summer, mixing water from the paddling pool with soil to make a mud pack. This she rubbed into her skin with all the enjoyment of an adult rubbing in a favourite body cream.

We use food to communicate, and children can let us know a lot by their acceptance or refusal of food. One little boy in Kenya taught me an enormous amount when I had to feed him regularly. This young fellow was in hospital being treated for worms (which had nearly killed him). He had cerebral palsy, so that even when he was able to eat again and had a gargantuan appetite, it had to be a slow affair. He rarely used speech (for emotional reasons), but was a very communicative boy. The hospital he was in was run by Asians, so he was trying out quite a number of new foods. I have to admit that I thought feeding him was just a matter of getting the food into his mouth and waiting for him to be ready for the next mouthful, but I soon found out how hopelessly and stupidly wrong I was!

The direction of his gaze showed me what part of the meal he wanted. So, once we had established that he liked something I would offer it to him again and then be surprised and irritated when he screwed up his nose and tightened his little mouth. 'But you just tried it and liked it!', I'd complain . . . until it dawned on me that he was not telling me he didn't like it, he was telling me he preferred a mouthful of something different at that point. I'd forgotten that as we eat we are constantly making choices of whether we want, for example, the rice on its own, or some vegetables with it, or meat on its own, and so on. I'm glad our relationship was good enough for him to feel he could assert himself in that way, for two reasons. The first is that he was so weak that it must have been good for his self-esteem to be able to control something. The second is that I would have learnt nothing (and his meal times would have been very boring for both of us), had he just let me shovel in what I felt like, in the order that suited me.

Essentially what I am saying is that by noticing *everything* we do and being willing to experiment with change, and being alert to our children's reactions, we can assist them in critical ways not only to communicate, but also to feel good about themselves.

If, however, our children are being taught artificial methods of communication (sometimes called Augmentative Systems), like Makaton or Bliss, it is vital that we demand to be taught as well, and use this method as much as possible with our children. We may feel embarrassed about this and learning may feel difficult for all sorts of reasons, yet learn we must if we are to ensure that our children can communicate with us and not just with other, less significant people. Makaton do sell Parent and Carer Information Leaflets to introduce you to the system for both younger and older children (see Resource List page 201).

Deaf children

In a mainly hearing society, the value placed on speech as the primary means of communication is very great indeed. The value attached to speech as the mainstream vehicle for self-expression and communication faces families with deaf children time and time again, placing pressure on them to recognise that society may not ordinarily consider a child as having a complete and acceptable role within the community unless they speak. An oralist approach grounds deaf children in a set of assumptions about equality and sameness that assigns disability to them: deaf children are basically oppressed by oralism because of its very insistence on conformity and uniformity.[1]

There are still professionals willing to swear on oath that teaching your child sign language will be like cutting them off from the rest of the world, since so few people know sign language. Speaking both as a one-time educational psychologist and as a friend of several deaf people, I would say this is an extremely dangerous attitude. It is absolutely critical to a child's development that if they can acquire language, they do. Children who are taught sign language initially get that chance, at a rate that makes sense, given the child's genetic predisposition to language acquisition. If we insist on forcing deaf children to lip-read, listen through earphones and speak (or more accurately make noises they can't hear and shape their mouths around those noises) they acquire frustratingly few words. Their entire education depends on good language acquisition, but so does their relationship with others. It is critical that if we don't already know sign language, we learn it with them or before them, at evening classes for instance. Good schools, speech and language therapists, or peripatetic teachers for deaf children use total communication. This is about employing any and every method to communicate with a child, using perhaps signed English, speech and finger spelling, and face and body language.

As Beazley and Moore point out in the study quoted above, parents get caught in the crossfire of professionals arguing about the best method of teaching for deaf children and this causes enormous distress. They quote one woman as follows:

> **Helen:** The most important thing is that [families] try anything to communicate and don't listen to professionals. Do what *you* think is best for *you* because you and your child won't suffer so much if you can communicate.

Quite apart from anything else, as long as the family learns sign language (and I should point out that it is great fun and that hearing children tend to take to it like ducks to water) if your child has only the command of sign language and nothing else, the truth is they can get along. In the first place there is a vast deaf community out there using sign language. In the second place, a child who uses sign language confidently and feels good about themselves, who has (because of having a language to base it on) been able to learn to read and write, will in fact always be able to make themselves understood. It seems to me that hearing professionals in the deaf world have often viewed sign language in the same way that non-disabled people view a wheelchair. To them, these things are terrible restrictions, but to the people who use them they represent freedom.

The severe implications of not having any language are brought home by the mother previously quoted, talking about the time her deaf daughter had to go into hospital for an operation on her ears.

> **Helen:** They came round to give her the pre-med and she didn't understand exactly what was happening . . . I'd tried already, but without sign language I couldn't even remotely communicate the problem to her or what was going to happen, except that she was going to be put to sleep and they were going to do something to her ears . . . By the time they reached Katy, they had run out of girl's night-gowns and they had a pair of boy's blue pyjamas. And first of all she looked at those and 'I'm not putting those on' and then they said 'Oh, she'll have to take her pants off', and the idea of taking her pants off was not on. And she screamed and she had a complete hysterical fit. She bit me, she kicked me and she had to be given two pre-meds to calm her down enough . . . And if she'd had sign language it just wouldn't have happened.'

A good resource is *You Choose* by Margaret Kennedy, a book created for deaf children to teach some of the safety messages others have written for hearing children.[2]

Other communication methods

It is not appropriate to discuss here *all* the different methods of communication open to disabled children, but do be aware that computers are revolutionising this critical area of our children's lives. For example, staff in a Family Centre in Leicester are using computers with abused children and have found that it seems to make it much, much easier for the children to let them know what has been happening, and how they feel – especially older children for whom play is no longer appropriate.

So don't be afraid of pushing for these or any other methods of communication, if you think they might help your child. If we think our child would communicate more, given a method suitable to them, we need not wait for someone else to suggest an appointment with a speech and language therapist. We can just make that request to our doctor or school ourselves, and be ready to explain what it is that makes us think our child could communicate more given the opportunity. This needs saying because the subtleties of how our children communicate may not be immediately obvious and, after all, even the most able children can be intimidated into silence (whether that is the silence of the mouth or the silence of the body), by a new environment or new person.

Where English is a second language

There are some significant difficulties for families who speak a language other than English at home, because their children will be taught an English based communication system at school, or by speech and language therapists. Parents in this situation may have to be very assertive to ensure that they do not become cut off from their children, and the children from their families.

Where pictures are used, parents could request that adjustments be made to suit cultural differences. For instance, Makaton now has some resources for Urdu, Punjabi, Gujurati and Hindi speaking families (see Resource list for details). Equally, when pictures are used with words underneath, someone could add the words in the first language, so that parents can make use of the system and the child can communicate both inside and outside of the family. Obviously, parents may have to make up some pictures for words not found in English, or signs for words or concepts not covered by British Sign Language.

Although there certainly are bilingual children with learning difficulties, the demands of learning two languages may mean a lowering of the achievement in each language to a point which is problematic for the child. In this situation, parents of children with learning difficulties may find it helpful to discuss with the whole family new strategies for including their child. For instance, if the rest of the family are bilingual, they might be happy to talk in English in the presence of their disabled child, but revert back to their first language in that child's absence.

Probably some local education authorities are doing more than others to make communication systems as inclusive as possible and parents may do well to contact others in different parts of the country for examples of good practice.

Making use of speech and language therapists

Many parents receive little information about the range of professions to which they can turn for help. The use of speech and language therapists, for example, is less common than physiotherapists, but they can play a vital role in teaching communication skills not just to the child, but also to their carers and teachers. They know how to get children to use speech muscles and mechanisms, and should also be able to work out the best communication system for your child if speech is not an option. They can help children who can speak but have a specific language disorder. It has to be said that they are sometimes not brought in to help with a child when they should be, and on the other hand, that they may underestimate a child's ability to communicate. But where there is a good working relationship between them and the schools, such difficulties are easily overcome (cutbacks notwithstanding). It should be possible to get a telephone number for a local speech and language therapy department from the Social Services (ask if they have a Child Development team because that's where they might be) and/or from the education authority. It is also possible to get a referral to a speech and language therapist through a GP or hospital consultant.

Child protection vocabulary

Society encourages us to think of physically disabled children as asexual. For some of us, it is very hard to imagine our children having consenting sexual relationships, and we use this to help us out of the difficulty of teaching our children even the basics. Whereas most of us teach our non-disabled children vocabulary for private parts of the body, whether we use family terms (like 'flower' or 'Mary' for vagina) or clinically correct terms like penis, many of us have failed to do this with our disabled children, putting them at great risk. Where a child has speech and language they should be taught the same terms as their brothers and sisters.

In those cultures where there is no such teaching until quite an advanced age, parents might like to consider the different circumstances and needs of their disabled children. Constraints on teaching about sex and sexuality usually arise out of religious or cultural beliefs about a minimum age or stage in life at which sexual relationships are acceptable. What needs to be taken into consideration with disabled children, however, is that there is a significant danger of their first sexual encounters being abusive ones, rather than consenting ones. Without a vocabulary even to refer to the parts of the body that have been interfered with, the child may be utterly silenced. It may be a matter for individual families to consider; it may be a subject for discussion with local religious or cultural leaders. At least if the subject is aired, it is a step towards protecting the child.

What we have to remember in all this is that non-disabled children can, and mostly do, pick up words and ideas from their peers, regardless of what we do as their parents. Many people can remember learning their first sexual vocabulary and ideas in a corner of the playground at school. Some of this may be harmful, some protective. With our disabled children, however, this kind of opportunity for unsupervised 'behind the bike-shed' conversations may not exist. Whilst in some respects that may be a relief, in others it is undoubtedly a cause for concern, for our children may be left much less 'streetwise' than their non-disabled counterparts and therefore much more vulnerable.

This can be massively exacerbated if the child is using an artificial or augmentative communication system, for these have mostly lacked even the basic terms with which the child can assert themselves, let alone terms for sexual body parts or abusive acts. This is now changing. If you think about it, most of our youngsters have learnt some version of 'go away and leave me alone' by the age of three to four; now it might be a version they have learnt from their friends, like 'piss off', of which we do not approve, but it can still serve to give the child a coat of armour. There is no system of which I am aware, provided to children using non-verbal communication (other than BSL) that provides such a concept. This *has* to be dangerous, not least because it heightens the child's sense of vulnerability.

This is another reason to be very familiar with the system of communication open to our children; we need to know whether or not it contains this aspect of vocabulary and if not, discuss with our child's school how to create signs or symbols and teach these to the child in an appropriate way. (Chailey Heritage, a Health Service provision in East Sussex, has done this, so that the children in their care who can use augmentative communication are not left stranded when it comes to communicating about sex, sexuality, and abuse.)

Of course we may have some work to do to become comfortable about discussing sexuality, because some of us may have had parents who were deeply uncomfortable about the subject themselves, and this in turn can make it hard for us to address with our own children. But it must be worthwhile if it can help the child tell us about abuse as soon as it occurs, and because it does appear that children prefer to learn about such matters from their parents. Besides, we too stand to benefit from overcoming our own shyness and inhibitions.

Clearly for children whose communication is involuntary only, this is not an option. What we then have to do is be willing to think the unthinkable. We have to be willing to consider the possibility of abuse if we are unable to come up with any other explanation for regular screaming, or other signs of distress, and to note any patterns, symptoms, or other behavioural changes, so that others can investigate the possible causes.

It has to be said that the story of Christy Nolan is an inspiring one. He was born with severe cerebral palsy and has never been able to speak. Nevertheless his mother always read to him and he listened avidly to the radio and watched TV. His mother managed to persuade her local school to have him in the classroom, but it was she who finally worked out a way in which he could express his own thoughts. She had a typewriter and she devised a way of attaching a stick to his head so he could press down the letters. To her absolute amazement, words poured out. By the time he was 13 he had written his first book of poetry – poetry so astonishing in the richness of its vocabulary that it took the academic world by storm. He entered university to study English long before his peers and has piled up literary honours ever since.[3]

This should not be taken to mean that if our child can't do this, they, or we, are failing! Christy Nolan is exceptional and no one knows how he acquired some of his vocabulary. The moral is simply that no one knows what a person can communicate until they are given the chance. It is not wildly different from Benjamin Zephaniah, another celebrated poet. He is a black Jamaican who began making up poetry to dub over music, when music producers couldn't afford to pay for fully developed music and song on both sides of a record. But he couldn't read or write when his first book of poetry was published! The point is that through the records, others were excited enough to write his poetry for him. He said in a radio interview that it was hearing himself described in a programme as a writer, rather than as a poet, that drove him to evening classes to learn to read and write. The issue, then, is not the method of communication, it is being able to communicate.

I appreciate that what we may have to do to maximise our communication with our children might feel like waving goodbye to yet *more* time and more energy, when these are already stretched to capacity. But in fact, when communication with our children is poor, it means a great deal of lost time as our children misbehave in their efforts to get us to 'hear' what they want us to know. I do believe it is a 'stitch-in-time' kind of investment for which we may be eternally grateful at some later stage.

Some tips on how to improve our own communication skills

Be prepared to play! Remember children learn a great deal through play. More importantly, when we play we are entering their world, not making them operate in ours. I find with my daughters that I often feel that I have been whisked off to another planet because they take no notice of me. It seems as though I could be hanging off the light shade and screaming and they would still be too absorbed in whatever fantasy they have created to realise I exist. My only hope of penetrating this soundproof barrier is to listen to the game, and work out a way of joining in, knitting into it what I am wanting to communicate. So I might need to say something like 'Mummy bear, will you come to the bathroom now and show your baby bear how to clean her teeth' – and suddenly I am flesh and blood again.

But we may want to be picking up messages, rather than giving them, and then joining in games can give us an enormous amount of information. Play therapists, of course, depend on being able to interpret children's play, but you don't have to be a trained professional for play to be useful to you. You can spot anything the child plays at over and over again. They are either trying to learn something by practising or they are trying to work out something that has caused them distress. I remember doing therapeutic work with a young girl in her school. The only space the school could offer was the library. I soon noticed that on every occasion this child would go unerringly to one particular book (which was never in the same place twice) and look at it. This was a small book about cows and how they give milk and had pictures of the calf suckling from its mother. It became obvious that she was communicating her desperate need for nurturing by her own mother, who found demonstrating affection really difficult.

Each of us has ways in which we are particularly effective at communicating over and above speech. Some of us enjoy singing. If so, sing! It may grab our child's attention in a way that speaking does not. Other people like drawing. Drawing for – and possibly with – our children may make communication open up dramatically. Really, there are a million possibilities if we can be flexible and daring. Remember, children aren't interested in our singing being perfectly in tune, or our drawing being art school standard; they are interested in the content. True enough, if we sing out of tune or draw a dog that looks more like a duck they might derive enjoyment from that; it is very empowering to see adults for once attempting something and not doing very well. Even so, they won't be critical or contemptuous, unless that is the way we have treated them.

Whatever our talents, we can use them for communication. All we have to do is work out ways of using our skills for communication purposes, and we are away. Everyone can get a thrill from inventiveness and, ultimately, understanding each other better.

Chapter Three

Intimate Care

Children who need intimate care face one of the highest levels of risk of abuse, whether it is within the family, from other carers or in institutions. Quite simply, the need for intimate care opens an enormous power gap between the child and the adult at the same time as giving the adult access to the child's body.

What exactly is intimate care? It's one of those terms we all feel we understand and yet struggle to define. Part of the reason for this is that what seems intimate to one person does not to another, so we cannot begin by assembling a list of activities and working out a definition on the basis of those. Looking at the factors involved in our personal assessments of whether or not care is intimate will help us.

For a start there are developmental issues. As very young children we need, accept and take for granted that others will help us with nearly every task. As small creatures, this requires close contact, sometimes skin to skin, sometimes not. We have no concept of acceptable or unacceptable, appropriate or inappropriate, private or public. No baby minds the world seeing its bottom as it is cleaned. But as we grow older, we are expected to learn what parts of our bodies we may or may not show to others.

First of all 'others' become anyone of the opposite sex, except within some families. Then they may be anyone outside of the immediate family, regardless of gender – except in certain situations like changing rooms, and excepting doctors when (hopefully) we are accompanied by our parents. Then as sexual adults (or teenagers) 'others' shrink so that in cultures where flirting is acceptable, we may show more of our bodies to potential partners, and all of our bodies to our sexual partners. But, of course, which parts of our body must be kept hidden varies culturally, as do the transitions in terms of 'others' and specific situations.

There are also variations in who is normally allowed access to our bodies, and to which parts. This even relates to some non-touch activities, especially in areas where respect and intimacy are closely related. Thus there are cultures in which it is deemed inappropriate for a woman to look a man in the eye. To do so is disrespectful at least, and flirtatious at most. In some cultures the gender of the person having access to your body after infancy is clearly laid down, in others it is not. Again, it is not just about what others may or may not see, it is also about what others may or may not touch, and with what. I committed a terrible faux pas in Malaysia once. I was on a tour with Graeae theatre company and we had learnt that one must shake hands only with the right hand, which is considered the clean hand. I had remembered right through until our very last day, when I wished to show our driver that I had appreciated all his efforts – with no shared verbal language with which to express that. I shook hands right-handedly but then in an attempt to convey something extra I covered his hand with my left also. He snatched his hand away and wiped it desperately on his clothing. Not the sort of thanks he will want to remember! What is acceptable within any culture also tends to vary with gender. For example, women may accept attention to various parts of their bodies from quite a large range of other females, whereas men may accept it to their heads and nowhere else, from the barber and no one else!

One might say that each culture (and sub-culture, since, for example, teenage culture and adult culture are sometimes radically different) creates *intimacy boundaries or barriers* depending on age, gender and situation and that those boundaries are based on cultural ideas around respect. It is, then, no surprise that in cultures like the white English culture, where respect is now almost universally to be earned, not given automatically, the intimacy boundaries are the least restrictive.

So, within the dictates of our own cultures and sub-cultures, we develop our individual sense of intimacy barriers. They change as we grow older – through childhood, adolescence, adulthood and old age. They change according to our movement through sub-cultures. Also they change according to our personal experiences. Someone who has not only moved through sub-cultures but also amongst other cultures may either develop greater flexibility in where they place their intimacy barriers, or go the other way and become more rigid. Someone who has had an abusive experience will often erect more intimacy barriers. For example one woman I know was raped. Since that time she has never worn a skirt again, but covers her legs completely with trousers. Someone who has been repeatedly abused throughout childhood may drop most intimacy barriers (or perhaps has never been allowed to develop them), which is one aspect of why so many abused youngsters end up as prostitutes.

Does this help us define intimate care? Well, we could draw it together and suggest that, after babyhood at least, intimate care is help that crosses normal intimacy barriers in that person's culture and sub-culture, regardless of personal experience. Since we may never know what the personal experiences may have been, however, any care may be felt to be intimate by a particular individual.

Thus for the Kikuyu tribe in Kenya, the bedroom occupied by a married couple is the one room in the house into which you may not go without invitation. Someone who has to go into this room then, perhaps to give care to a sick mother, is crossing the intimacy barrier just by being there. After that, this mother may not feel that tidying her hair, for example, is in any way intimate (though another might).

Such a definition is helpful if only because it forces us to be clear about developmental stages and gender issues and to enquire about cultural norms. However, it is limited because those barriers were not drawn up with disabled people in mind, and many people delivering intimate care do so as if the disabled person has no intimacy barriers at all. This is evident in quotes from two women attending a residential school for blind and partially sighted children.

> There was a total lack of privacy, you were all together in these big rooms, all got dressed together, all in the bathrooms together. Even the toilets had no locks on the door, you had to sit there and yell 'Somebody's in' right up until you were 16.

> We had to queue up waiting for a bath, there was never any privacy. They even used to (I don't like to say this) make us stand in our pyjama bottoms and lift our arms to check that we had washed everywhere. They were very strict about it. That was when we were 15 or 16.[1]

I quote these to illustrate that ideas of intimacy are thrown out *not* just for the most dependent of our children, but often for any and all disabled children.

Accepting the fact that each person has a different perception of intimacy is vital. If individual experience can make something feel intimate to me that does not feel intimate to you, then we all have to create far greater sensitivity. Ruth Marchant created some very interesting exercises around this subject, listing activities and asking whether or not people thought they were intimate care.[2] There are always some who unhesitatingly say that tying other people's shoelaces is not intimate, yet doing so brings your eyes in line with the other person's genitals if they are sitting down, and so it could be felt to be intimate. Equally if you have been blessed with smelly feet, your intimacy barriers are going to extend out much further than someone who does not have that problem! Again, some people are confident that helping someone on with their coat is not intimate. Cultural issues aside, they are often reminded by women that if it involves doing buttons up, then the helper's hands can be extremely close to a woman's breasts. In other words it is not in any way safe to judge intimacy according to what does or does not seem intimate to you.

How does all of this relate to disabled children who have gone beyond babyhood but still need some or many aspects of intimate care on a daily, and perhaps permanent basis? Intimacy barriers have been defined largely by and for young adults or adults who are non-disabled. They have almost no bearing on the lived experience of many disabled young people and cannot help them make sense of their world. For some children, it is hard to conceive that they have a concept of private and public, for *many* people may have direct access to the genital areas of their bodies, as well as performing various other tasks which may be less acutely intimate but nevertheless cross normal intimacy barriers.

We can only begin to appreciate the full meaning of this by thinking about how many people had access to our bodies, for things like bathing, when we were children (unless we ourselves were disabled and needed intimate care). For most of us, about three people were the maximum who ever performed such duties; usually our mother or father, and perhaps an older sister. For disabled children this can be more like 17 in the space of a week, though for those with the most complex impairments it can rise to as many as 40.[3] It is not difficult to imagine how this must feel. Not only does the impact of all these people make developing a concept of privacy extremely difficult, it makes communicating ideas like 'It's your body' nigh on impossible – yet such ideas are an important part of helping disabled children to become more assertive. It also, in combination with the plethora of professionals that might enter a child's life, makes the notion of a stranger inconceivable. Nearly everyone is a stranger, but nearly everyone has instantly to be trusted and given access to your body. Children sometimes respond by cutting off from both physical and emotional feelings, which can leave them more vulnerable than ever.

The problems surrounding the issue of intimate care then are manifold. These difficulties are further complicated by the question of who is to deliver intimate care. If you have not had to have intimate care since you were a child, try imagining that some accident has befallen you and now you will have to stay in bed for three weeks, having absolutely everything done for you. Who would you choose? Some of us instantly choose spouses or partners. Others choose mothers or daughters or sisters (occasionally brothers). What is of interest is the criteria we use to make these choices. Some of it relates to social roles (the woman as nurturer, for example), much of it relates to trust, and much to familiarity. But it also

relates to other aspects of one's relationships. Now, what
if your need for intimate care is not going to be
temporary, but permanent? Most people's choice of who
they would choose to deliver intimate care changes
dramatically when they are thinking long-term. Trust
seems to take a secondary place and what takes over is
all about the power balances and imbalances that such
care might create.

Generally when people think about who would look
after them long-term, they do not consider the possibility
that they might be abused. What is a consideration is the
desire not to be a burden on the carer. This fear
demonstrates the underlying feeling of vulnerability, of
no longer seeing oneself as an equal. So, for example,
those choosing their spouses to care for them for three
weeks often feel that, on a permanent basis, this would
shift their relationship too far away from a reasonable
balance of power between them. Or those choosing
family members feel that the amount of work involved
for their chosen person would be too great and would
spoil their lives, and therefore the relationship.

What does that mean for those children for whom
long-term intimate care is indeed a reality? It reminds us
that they have *absolutely no choice* about who is
involved. Whether or not they love or feel loved by a
person is irrelevant (in terms of choice); whether or not
they trust a person is irrelevant; whether they feel a
person will use or abuse the power imbalance is
irrelevant. They get who they are given.

Admittedly adults asked about their choices would
tend to move to employed strangers once they had
discounted their 'temporary choices', but many are
aware that this is almost no choice at all. In the ideal
situation we would have enough money to be able to hire
and fire as we wished, with the absolute ideal being that
we found two people who were perfect and who could

divide the work happily between them, with never a day off for sickness. But of course that is cloud cuckoo land for almost all of us and the harsh reality is that we are often dependent on people sent by our local Social Services, or the agency to whom they give the work. Some local authorities and some agencies do accept us ringing up and asking for someone to be replaced. Others do not. But at least if these strangers are helping us at home we can observe them and we can fight to have them replaced as necessary. The critical issue is that we, and they, are only a tiny proportion of the total number of carers our children will get, especially once they are of school age. I believe it would be horrifying for some of us to count up all the nurses, health visitors, school helpers, respite carers and so on, who have had access to our children's bodies. How must it feel to our children?

Remember that even if absolutely every one of these people handled our children with total respect, they would of necessity handle them differently. Each person comes with their own religious, cultural and personal make-up. Some are nearly always light-hearted. Some are nearly always dour. Some are warm, some are clinical. Some believe disabled children should be pushed to do as much as possible for themselves, others believe that is cruel and that the children should be given as much help as they need or ask for. We will go into some of this in more detail, but for the moment, let's just acknowledge how incredibly hard it must be for even the most flexible human being to deal with this variety. Not only must the child accommodate each person's different ways, they must try to disentangle who they actually are from the images projected onto them by each individual.

This was hard enough for me as an adult receiving home care to help me with my daughters. Yet our children have to deal with people who may be undressing them, toileting them, washing them, clothing them or feeding them. If you never understood the intimacy of being fed (other than those moments when lovers share a spoonful!) try feeding your partner or best friend for five minutes, and getting them to do the same for you. Now imagine having to accommodate to one person who likes to 'let you take your time' so you are left waiting anxiously for the next mouthful, and another who believes in shoving it down in short order. Imagine there is one who puts salt on your food whether or not you want it and another who never thinks you might want seasoning or sauces. Essentially we are asking our children to do the most extraordinary emotional contortions, the equivalent of those amazing, double-jointed people who can tie themselves up in knots.

So receipt of intimate care is problematic for our children regardless of the professionalism of the people involved. In addition, they are often receiving this care not in our homes where, hopefully, it can be monitored, but in various kinds of institutions, where all sorts of unhealthy practices can, and too often do, develop. One of the girls with whom I work recently started her periods. She was horrified when her school helpers appeared in masks and gloves to change her sanitary towels! She succinctly queried, 'Do they put masks and gloves on to change their own?' Gloves we can understand in this day and age, but masks? When this girl's parents challenged the school, via the Head of Special Educational Needs, they found it was an uphill battle. This woman wholeheartedly backed her staff. It was only the equal refusal of the father to budge that led to a compromise: other helpers were found who would not insist on masks.

This is an instance of emotionally abusive practice and is certainly the thin end of the wedge. In a focus group run by the Council for Disabled Children the young people also had something to say about residential care.

> I went to the accessible loo and it was just too small.
> If I got in, the door was open. When I get dressed, it
> can take a long time and lots of space. I don't like
> undressing in front of other people, they stare. When I
> said this about our [residential] school, they were very
> surprised. But they asked the others and they said they
> didn't like it either. We have curtains now.

Full marks to the institution for listening and acting on
what they heard. But why on earth were they surprised?
Another youngster added:

> Locks on doors and privacy. Couldn't people knock
> before they come in? You're not public property
> because you're away from home. Do people go
> barging in on Prince William at Eton? I bet they don't.

I was told by one group of young adults about various
abusive practices in relation to intimate care that used to
take place in the residential health authority school they
attended. Choosing their own clothes was never a
possibility, but worse, one worker would always dress a
particular little girl in dresses that were too short so that her
bottom was on show. So severe were the repercussions of
voicing any discontent (this same little girl was also denied
the toilet for five hours because she had been 'uppity') that
there was never any question of her complaining to anyone.
Another little boy was left on the toilet for several hours –
he remembers it as nine hours – because, he reckoned, the
member of staff who took him went off for a tea break in
the middle and forgot about him!

Improving on intimate care

There is a certain amount we can do at home and we
shall look at this first. Then we will address what we can
require of the institutions attended by our children.

Whilst our children are very young, and of course later

if they have fairly profound learning difficulties, intimate care tasks are wonderful opportunities for all sorts of learning – from both the child's perspective and ours. We are communicating by how we touch the child and how we respond to them. When they are happy and wide awake we can be playful; when they are tired or grumpy we may need to be efficient but gentle and warm. It is very important, though, that we also talk to them as we perform these tasks. In particular it is important that we let them know what we are going to do before we do it. This performs many functions. In the first place it is part of 'bringing the world into being' for the child, by naming objects and actions. In the second place it provides stimulation and makes the task more interesting. That is especially helpful if the child doesn't like the procedure. In the third place it communicates to the child that we value them as a human being; they are not just a lump of flesh we have to wash or dress. Finally it provides the child with opportunities to help us, by co-operating.

I recall helping a friend of mine with her baby who had brittle bones. By the time she was five months old, if her mother or I told her we were going to take her cardigan off, she would just lift her shoulder a little bit to ease the process. If a child can't do this much, knowing what is about to happen may allow them to relax so that the procedure can be less of a 'fight'. We can, and should, also explain why we do things. Again the primary reason is to help the child make sense of their world. Having things done to you is frightening enough without being bewildered as to why it is happening. Those of us who have ever been in hospital can, I'm sure, vouch for that. The doctor or nurse who explains the reason for a procedure before doing it, even when we have no choice in the matter, feels like an ally; someone who respects us.

So we can talk to our children and remind them how precious they are to us; we can talk about the objects we are using; we can talk about the sequence of events. We can take the opportunity to help them learn about new things – left and right, for example, by saying, I'm going to put your left sock on first, then your right sock.' We can talk about our relationship with them, how they seem to be feeling or how we are feeling. It is particularly useful to address how they react to what happens. If they cry when they come out of the bath, we can say, 'Oh, you don't like coming out, do you? I'm sorry but you would start to get cold if I left you in any longer.' The value of this lies in part in acknowledging that they don't like it and that we have noticed. It becomes more important when, in response to what we have noticed, we can change something.

Let's take the opposite scenario; the child who cries when they are placed in the bath. We might say, 'You don't like that first moment in the bath, do you? Do you want to feel the water with your hand first, before you get in?' It doesn't matter that they can't answer. It matters that we can try this out and continue if it helps, and try something else (like letting them watch a toy floating in it first). This reinforces for the child the *value* in communicating and gives them an increased sense of being in control.

Much of how this relates to child protection should already be clear, and the more the child enjoys intimate care tasks with us, the better foundation there is for them to make it clear when someone is performing these tasks in ways they don't like. We can maintain many aspects of this approach to intimate care as our children get older.

Routines

If you think about it, as adults in charge of our own intimate care, we use any number of routines. Consider when you take a shower or have a bath. Most of us wash the various parts of our bodies in the same sequence every time. Even when we clean our teeth we tend to start in the same place and move the brush around our mouths in a certain, unvarying pattern. When we get dressed or undressed, we also tend to have a sequence of what goes on or comes off first, what next, and so on. My sequence and yours may be different, but we all have our own way of doing things. Why? Well, these are tasks that must be performed every day, some several times a day, but we have better things to think about than an endless stream of new, extremely minor decisions. Imagine how tiring it would be to have to work out afresh each morning whether to put your socks on after your pants; whether to put your right foot into your trousers first, or your left. Most of us develop our sequences for inconsequential reasons, but we stick with them because it frees us to pay attention to other, more important, or more interesting things. Our routines give us a sense of security. This is always true, whether it's the routine pattern of the day, or of intimate tasks.

In addition to talking our children through intimate care tasks, therefore, we need, for their sake and ours, to develop some routines. Obviously, from what has already been said, flexibility and therefore the ability to change the routine in response to the child is important, but these changes to routine should still be fairly predictable. Routines help us, as parents and carers, in as much as they ease the workload, and ease the amount of time we have to spend working out solutions to the millions of problems, small and large, that arise on a daily basis. They are helpful to our children also (and critical for most youngsters with autism), in as much as their predictability helps the child to have some sense of order, if not control. But control does come into it too – our children will often protest loudly if we have missed an element of the routine, and that can be very helpful. If the child recognises our routines, that tells us something about them (their capacity to recognise and learn sequences, for example) and tells them that they deserve some order in their lives.

With this basis, our children are in as strong a position as possible when it comes to receiving intimate care from others. If they can't describe the routines themselves, we can, and we can require that they be followed as closely as possible. We can also require that if they are altered we should be told, and given reasons, if not actually consulted.

Now this maintenance of routines is more critical for some aspects of intimate care than others. Thus, when a child needs manual evacuation of the bowel, routine is essential for the child's health. At the same time, since toileting is so open to abuse, it is vital that the child has the best possible chance of detecting variation from the norm. Regular skin care is vital to children who have eczema, to prevent bleeding and infections, and to black children who more easily suffer from dry skin.

Routine is also critical for certain children in relation to particular procedures. So, for example, children with physical impairments may be absolutely dependent on their garments being put on starting with one particular limb. Or a child who walks with calipers may be unable to even get the caliper on if their legs are not massaged beforehand. Blind people of all ages depend heavily on routine, whether it is the routine of where objects are placed, or of journey sequences which must be memorised because landmarks and destinations cannot be seen. A child with physical impairments who is also blind, lives in a world that is capable of delivering too many shocks. Speaking before touching such a child is absolutely crucial to their sense of safety, and sticking to routines will minimise the nasty surprises. And of course, however little we know of autism, we know that routine makes a terrifying world somewhat less frightening. If this is true about such things as who sits where at the table, how much more so in the close encounters of intimate care.

If we can establish routines at home that ease the passage of the day in general, and the activities involved in intimate care in particular, we owe it both to our children and to those who care for them, to pass on information about those routines. Any person or institution that is not interested in this information is not interested in our children and that should concern us a great deal. On the other hand, any considerate person entering our child's life would appreciate learning all they can about routines, to smooth the transitions between home and other places – and to make the job easier for themselves. Let's face it, a child confronted with completely new routines is likely to be tense, if not downright miserable, and that makes pleasant delivery of intimate care infinitely harder.

If others can't follow certain aspects of the routines, then this should be explained to the child whenever and in whatever way makes most sense for this child. But it is vital that the carer or institution should also develop their own clear routines, so that at least the child can relate a particular routine to a particular place.

Choice

A constant theme throughout this book is the emphasis on empowerment. Choice is a key element of power, alongside the information on which to base that choice. One of the great fallacies of modern life is the idea that we are more in control because we have so much choice. Take mobile phones, for instance. Some might say we have great choice because there are so many different companies, different tariffs and so on. The reality is that there is so much complicated information, that to make an informed choice one would probably have to take a calculator along to compute the advantages and disadvantages of each company's offers. Instead, we allow any number of other factors, from advertising to our energy levels at the moment of decision ('Do I just want to buy the damn thing, or have I got what it takes to stuff in any more information from any more shops?'), to make the choice for us. Empowerment depends on having digestible information, being given realistic choices, and then having those choices honoured, or put into effect. So how does this relate to intimate care?

Again it is useful to remember the kinds of choices most of us can take for granted. We can determine whether or not we would like to have a hot bath if we are feeling stiff or stressed. We can choose which particular set of underwear or outer clothing suits our mood or circumstances. We certainly choose the moment when we head for the toilet. It is not uncommon for all these choices to be denied to disabled children and adults. I recall a young friend of mine from whom I learnt a great deal. She was paralysed from the neck down following an operation, and had finally made it from a hospital to a hostel. She complained bitterly about bath-time and the staff's absolute inability to take her wishes seriously.

But during her stay in the hospital too, staff were sometimes alarming in their dealings with her, especially in relation to intimate care. I remember her very deliberately asking me to remain in the room when a particular nurse came to change her catheter (the tube that drains urine from the bladder). The nurse did the job with hardly a word to my friend. When she thought she had finished, my friend said, 'I'm sorry, but you'll have to do something, it's twisted.' The nurse looked at her with a mixture of astonishment and anger and retorted, 'How could you possibly know? You've got no feeling!' Perhaps because I was there observing, however, she took it out – and discovered it was indeed twisted. As my friend explained to me later, although she had no sensation on her skin from the neck down, she did have some internal sensation. It was important for both of us that I honoured this unusual choice of remaining to witness one of life's least pleasant and most intimate of intimate care tasks. My friend had less of a battle on her hands, and I learnt a big lesson about not making assumptions.

We can, then, offer many more choices to disabled children than we currently do. Perhaps, if we asked, they would choose a different place or time for incontinence pad changes. Perhaps they would vary the temperature of their drinks. Maybe we could occasionally offer them the sort of treats we give ourselves, like bubble baths. They may not only derive fantastic enjoyment from choosing their own clothes (both in the shops and on a daily basis), but also learn a huge amount in the process. Offering and acting on choices sends a respectful message; one that acknowledges them as equal human beings.

It *is* true that we can overburden a child with choices. We can do this in several ways, such as asking children to make choices on subjects too complicated for them emotionally, in terms of the possible long-term implications, or in terms of their experience. We can also overburden children by giving them too many choices, so that life becomes nothing but a series of decisions. After my children made a big fuss some time ago along the lines of 'I didn't want *that* cereal' I began to ask them what they did want every morning for breakfast. Right now they are tired of that and just tend to say 'You choose!' But that is okay. Life is like that. We sometimes have to learn by doing something to death before we are ready to move on.

One way to avoid the latter problem is by learning the usual choices and then taking them for granted until or unless a different choice is made. We could check after a while by asking, 'Is this still what you want?' That same young friend that I already mentioned found it very difficult that staff at her hostel thought empowerment meant forcing residents to make and state the same decisions over and over, rather than learning at least some *general* preferences and sticking to them. This meant her life was reduced to utterly boring details far too much of the time.

When, perhaps as carers for other people's children, or maybe as parents whose children have been away from us in residential settings, we find a child who is overwhelmed by being offered choices, we must start with just one or two small things a day. Let the child get used to the idea of being given information and choice; introduce them gradually to the experience of being handed some control over their lives. If we rush in, requiring them to choose everything, it will be upsetting and they will long for the security of everything being done without consultation.

So, as with most things in life, there is a balance to be struck, but it isn't that hard if we listen to our children and treat them with respect.

Questions to ask institutions

Whilst most institutions these days have laid down Child Protection policy and procedures, few have Intimate Care policy and procedures. If they did, they could guard against too many staff having access to our children and they could maximise continuity of style and routine in intimate care tasks. This would take away a vast amount of stress for our children, but also be more comfortable for staff who are often left unguided. It would also mean that children could develop assumptions about how intimate care was going to be delivered and be able to alert someone when these processes were not being adhered to. It would make our children much, much safer. So ask the head or manager of the institution in question whether or not there is such a set of guidelines, and push for one strongly if there is not. If there is, of course, it should be shared with parents and children as well as being given to staff.

If there are such guidelines, what do they cover? Do they tell staff whether or not they can perform intimate care tasks alone? If so, and staff are permitted to work alone, what safeguards are in place to protect children? If not, how is the child's sense of privacy and dignity promoted? Do the guidelines address racial and cultural issues? Do they address the varying cultural rules around gender and different norms for intimate tasks?

One particular issue to watch out for is the myth that children will be safe as long as all intimate care is carried out by women. Whilst it is certainly true that most perpetrators, particularly of sexual abuse, are men, women also can and do commit abuse of all kinds. Jacqui Saradjian makes it clear that most of the women she studied targeted their own children.[4] Nevertheless nearly 20 per cent of all the victims were in fact unrelated to the women who abused them. Given that this is the case, we need to be sure that there is no complacency of the type that says, 'All perpetrators of abuse are men, therefore the children here are safe because we only employ women.' There are some institutions that have adopted a women only staff policy, but it is misguided not only because of the above myth, but also because women will not always be the appropriate carers for all children. Equally we must remember that boys are abused as well as girls.

If guidelines don't exist in writing, it is still worth asking these questions. How they are answered, as well as the content of the answers, should give you an accurate impression of the institution's attitude towards the children in its care. It is also wise to ask for a copy of their Child Protection policy and procedures. We don't have to be experts to glean some of the things we need to know from this document. We need to know, for example, whether or not an institution would tell us if our child had received intimate care from a suspected perpetrator, because, as Marchant and Page point out in *Bridging the Gap*, a child who receives intimate care from a suspected abuser is also at risk, and if they have received regular, unsupervised intimate care, then the risk is enormous.[5]

We also need to know what provision is made for our children to be able to contact us, without, if possible, supervision from staff. In other words, if our children are capable either of sending us written messages, or of using a telephone, is everything in place to make that possible? Essentially, if our children felt frightened or upset, would they be able to get in touch with us to let us know?

Handled in a respectful and thoughtful way, intimate care tasks need not simply represent danger for our children. They provide an opportunity for helping our children to communicate, to learn about themselves and others, and thereby establish a positive sense of their own identity. In later life they may also find that they can transfer what they learned about communicating with others to their own relationships. The hope is that through being listened to, as well as listening, our children will acquire self-knowledge and insight.

Chapter Four

Sexuality and Sexual Relationships

An important way of protecting our children from sexual abuse is to give them the information they need – ignorance is no protection at all. But we also need to recognise our children's right to a sexual life – to deny them that is a basic negation of their right to be treated as equals. It is also a denial of their emotional capacity to love and be loved.

There is a tremendous lack of recognition of disabled people's sexual development. When sexuality is acknowledged, it is usually in the context of vicious, negative stereotypes. Already we have touched on the classic stereotype of people with physical and sensory impairments as asexual, and people with learning difficulties as sex-mad monsters. We can assume that both ends of this particularly nasty stereotype are an expression of society's deepest fears of and disgust for disability. There the unstated belief that disabled people, of whatever ilk, should be prevented at all costs from having sexual relationships in case they have babies like themselves.

Many disabled people who have had children can testify to the incredible hostility and ignorance that must be faced and dealt with in order to have a child (though happily this is not everyone's experience). The organisation for disabled parents, Parentability, has endless stories from its members of the struggle just to proceed with a pregnancy, let alone be well supported by professionals and family throughout. In a paper called 'Doctor Doctor' Nasa Begum reported on disabled women's experiences of GPs.[1] Sharon, who is blind says:

> When I was pregnant with my first son I received a letter from the hospital asking me to attend the out-patients . . . I had no idea what it was about, but assumed it was a check-up of some sort. When I arrived I was told that a letter had been sent by someone (whose name could not be divulged), who had suggested that I should be offered an abortion. I was unable to ascertain who had written the letter but at this early stage only my GP knew I was pregnant.

And she added, in common with the experiences of many other disabled women:

> I have felt on each of my pregnancies . . . that I have been viewed as a freak. I was made to feel as if I was irresponsible and a cause for concern or that I was wonderful and an inspiration. I do not welcome either label.

But this is to spend time at, if you like, the end of the story, and we need to start at the beginning.

It is not insignificant that many people, because of the medical model of disability, and the publicity given to particular conditions like Muscular Dystrophy and Down's Syndrome, believe that most impairments have a genetic origin. This feeds the idea that if disabled people are allowed to have sexual relationships, they are bound to produce people with impairments. Now personally, of course, if that were the case, I would not have any great problem with it. However, that is not the point. Most impairments do *not* have a genetic origin and we should not confuse genetic causes with impairment at birth. There are many factors that can cause babies to be born with impairments: drug and alcohol abuse, physical assault on a pregnant mother; maternal malnutrition; some maternal illnesses like rubella; birth traumas and so on. The balance of proportions of those that do and those that don't arise genetically will swing around occasionally (for example the polio epidemic of the Fifties will have swung the pendulum hugely to the side of acquired impairments), but in general, the figures do not come down on the side of genetic causation. As Ruth Bailey observes:

> The first question usually asked, and answered, immediately after birth is 'Is the baby all right?' This question now dominates the early stages of pregnancy because most women now undergo some form of prenatal testing. Yet the number who will give birth to a disabled child is very small – less than 3 per cent . . . more than 90 per cent of childhood impairment occurs at or after birth and much is the result of environmental factors or accidents.[2]

So, with that misconception out of the way, we need to face fair and square the fact that unless our children sadly die young, they will develop sexually. Their sexual development may be delayed or uneven, but it will happen. Most will be capable of sexual feelings and most of sexual acts, whether or not they will ever be able to have *consenting* sex. This means we must think very carefully about how to promote that development in the most helpful way, how to acknowledge and defend their sexuality (whatever that may be), and how to support their sexual choices, if and when choices are made. I am extremely averse to the wholesale sterilisation of women with learning difficulties that has gone on in various countries around the world at various times. As Dick Sobsey says:

> They have been sterilised and denied the right to sexual expression and reproduction against their will . . . Not everyone considers these actions against people with disabilities to be abusive. Some of them have been permitted, even condoned, by law.[3]

Sterilising them does not protect them; it dehumanises them. There are many better options open to us if pregnancy and childbirth are truly out of the question and if not, we should direct ourselves to supporting the mother. I acknowledge that for those of us whose children will never have consenting sex, it will feel particularly hard to address this whole area, but if we wish to protect them as fully as possible, it's better thought about than not.

Given how abysmal most of our own sexual education has been, and bearing in mind that many of us will have had sexual experiences we would prefer to forget, we can forgive ourselves if we find this whole area difficult! But difficult and impossible are certainly not the same thing. Talking about how best to teach our children with someone we trust seems as good a starting point as any.

Our families will have varied enormously in terms of what was and wasn't talked about; who was allowed to talk to whom; terms used for genital areas and so on. If you had the good luck to grow up in a family where the subject was addressed with ease and confidence (albeit in culturally different ways) you probably will feel relatively confident about tackling the issue with your own children. Unfortunately most of us are not in this happy position. Many of our parents wouldn't discuss it. Some alluded to it in hushed or embarrassed tones; some grew angry at the mere mention of the issue; and some used the most weird and wonderful vocabulary which absolutely no one else had ever heard of (how about 'hamster' for vagina? The mind boggles!). One way or another, many of us have to shake off the dust of some rather weak parental models in order to tackle the issues more helpfully for our own children, particularly so for our disabled children.

When we have done that, and can take a look at the issues for our disabled children, we will need to ask ourselves many questions. The first step in teaching our children about sex is naming the body parts. There are plenty of dilemmas here, even if the child has speech and hearing. Do we use the terms our families used? Would anyone else understand them? If not, it may leave our children struggling to communicate effectively, should they suffer abuse. Do we use the clinical terms, like penis and vagina? All professionals will certainly understand these, but if we find ourselves uncomfortable with such medical terminology there is the danger that we may communicate that discomfort to our children, who could then feel very inhibited about addressing the topic. Equally, whatever terms we choose may not be the terms with which others, in whose care we leave our children, feel comfortable.

Once more we are drawn back to the need for the fullest communication between parents, carers, schools, and other people who look after our children on a regular basis. It is hopeless for the child if everyone washing their genital area gives it a different name. In particular, a child who cannot see or perhaps feel that area, can end up extremely confused about what there is, or isn't, down there!

If we have children who are using non-verbal systems

of communication, will we be able to persuade teachers or others to introduce sexual vocabulary at the right time to our children? Will we, for that matter, agree as to what the right time is? Reaching agreement about this might be difficult with just our partners, let alone anyone else.

As a single mother myself, one of the few benefits I revel in is *not* having to struggle with a partner over issues like this!

Explaining about acceptable and unacceptable behaviour

It is critical that we apply the same standards of acceptable behaviour to our disabled children as we do to non-disabled children. For example, we would automatically stop a non-disabled child from masturbating or showing their private parts in public. If a disabled child is not expected to follow the same social norms, they may be in danger because of the messages this sends to perpetrators of abuse. Inappropriate sexual behaviour can also be a sign of abuse. Indulging inappropriate behaviour on any grounds, whether it's 'But someone like him can't mean any harm' or 'Poor dear, it's the only pleasure she gets' is both irrational and dangerous. Regardless of the challenges involved in teaching what is socially admissible, we *must* attempt to do so and we must expect other carers in our children's lives to tackle it in the same way. Again consistency is essential. It is useless if a child learns that it's not okay to show their bottom at home, but they can do it in respite care. Not only do we need to let all other carers know what we are attempting to teach our children, we need to let them know how we are doing it. It is deeply confusing to a child to have one person kindly but firmly stopping them from masturbating in public and another slapping their hands and threatening them that they'll go blind if they carry on like that!

Once more, achieving that consistency is more easily said than done. In the first place there may be quite a bit of persuading needed. In the second, even if someone in charge of an institution, or perhaps a child's key worker in respite care, places an agreement with you, achieving this with all the people involved with our children is a daunting task. But we can rightfully demand maximum co-operation, especially from the heads of institutions.

If our children use a formal, non-verbal system of communication other than British Sign Language, Bliss or Makaton, we have a more formidable task on our hands because the vocabulary for so-called private body parts may be non-existent. In this instance we need to draw on the best professional allies we have encountered to ensure that such a vocabulary is developed, even if it is purely 'in house', that is peculiar to the institution in which it is originated. As long as all the children and all the staff and all the parents are made aware of it, the child will benefit enormously.

Sex Education

This is part of the national curriculum and our children have as much right to it, and as much need for it as anyone else. There are two separate aspects to sex education. The first is factual: what parts of our bodies do what and when, and how male and female bodies come together to produce babies. The other aspect is the moral or religious dimension. I am going to address the latter first, extremely briefly, dodging all the difficult issues, because this book is primarily about protection and also because the alternative would require writing another book!

Quite simply, it seems to me that we should present our children with our personal beliefs and standards concerning sex. These beliefs may be deeply rooted in our religion or culture. As these will be the values we teach our non-disabled children, so they should also be applied to our disabled children. So whatever we expect, in terms of moral behaviour, of our non-disabled children, we should also expect of our disabled children. Absolutely nothing else is respectful.

In terms of teaching factual information about sexual development, sexuality and sex acts, we need our children to understand as much as possible, to the maximum of their ability, if they are to have any chance at all of resisting sexual abuse. They will also be better equipped to disclose anything unpleasant if it should happen to them. We would be wise, therefore, to support anything the school attempts to this end, and to insist that every attempt is made to make the materials as accessible to our children as possible. Where this giving of information clashes with our cultural beliefs, we should try for the most constructive dialogue possible with the school. Some teaching materials aimed specifically at children with particular impairments have already been devised and used, such as the exercises in *Turning Points*, so it may not be a matter of having to start from scratch.[4]

Having a sex life

If we take this phrase in its broadest sense – having opportunities to enjoy one's sexuality – then we can help our children in many ways. Because the brute reality of life is that visibly disabled young people are less likely to be sought out as sexual partners, they need us in the first place to boost their morale by actively supporting them in the kinds of teenage activities that most young people are free to enjoy.

Even if their non-disabled peers exclude them from the teen-scene, we can encourage them. We can trail round shops helping them to choose whatever is the latest in teenage chic (assuming our pockets can stand this!) This can be fraught with difficulty, of course. I may betray my age when I say that as a teenager, 'A' line skirts were in fashion, and if there was one thing in the world which I could not possibly carry off, it was looking good with a straight skirt clinging to the outlines of my caliper! In this situation, the best support we can give our children will be in reassuring them that they can look just as good – and perhaps set the new trend – if they wear something a bit different. If someone in the family is good at dressmaking, then they and the youngster can have fun designing and making their own 'designer clothes'. A bit of creativity can also make an impossible dress or shirt possible after all. The teenage years are hard enough without feeling that our parents are co-conspirators in the plot to render us invisible, or downright unattractive, to those to whom we are attracted. Feeling good and looking good must be thought of as part of their protective cloak. This brings to mind one of the most damaging things I recall being said to a girl who used a wheelchair. She was advised to dress in black so that she could blend in with the chair and not be noticed!

There is no doubt that the above 'advice' would shock most sensitive people, but I believe it is not a million miles away from what some parents feel. In other words, we and our children have mostly had to endure so much endless staring and intrusive behaviour, that we do all sometimes wish we could become invisible, going where we wanted without attracting any attention at all. The desire to blend in, not stand out, comes from this pain. So if it is hard to see our non-disabled teenagers with green streaks in their hair or rings through their eyebrows, how much more so if our disabled young people wish to do the same? And yet in truth, if our young people do wish to take up these startling styles, we should be celebrating, for it means they can overcome the stares; they feel good enough about themselves to have no need at all to hide away. (I hope I can be this wise about my own children when the time comes!!!) It's not so different from my desire to paint climbing plants up my walking stick. If I have to use it, and others have to see it, let it be fun!

This all relates to acceptance by our peers. We are all attracted to people who appear to be enjoying themselves and if our young people can achieve this, then they also make a move in the direction of safety, by avoiding at least some aspects of isolation. This was well illustrated by another girl in Kenya, albeit at an earlier age. This child had spina bifida and, at the age of seven, had just acquired calipers and was learning to walk. Up till this point, non-disabled children had rarely played with her because, despite her quick mind and sunny disposition, she was limited to bottom shuffling, and they, of course, preferred to be more active. I showed some local craftsmen how to make her some parallel bars out of tree branches, and then showed her how to use them to walk. She grasped the possibilities quickly and screamed with delight as she rampaged up and down the length of the bars. Within minutes the other children, attracted by these joyous yells, came rushing to join her. It was a wonderful sight.

True enough, managing to see ourselves as physically attractive on our own terms is no easy thing, as we are all constantly exposed to the very limited ideal of female beauty promoted by the media. It *is* possible to take a very positive perspective. With different pieces of equipment, and differently designed bodies, disabled people have fashion opportunities that are not open to non-disabled people! Disabled models have recently appeared on the scene, posing for photos used in catalogues, and even taking over the cat-walks. It must be said that my mother managed to help me turn the fascism of fashion on its head. She acknowledged that I was never going to make Miss World, but by encouraging me to wear clothes that suited me, rather than those in fashion, she actually released me from fashion's clutches. I have always felt free to please myself in how I dress – which is much less stressful and a great deal less expensive! If this appears to be frivolous, it is anything but.

All this is relevant to all our children. We can be daring on behalf of our children, offering them a wide range of clothes to choose from or decorations for their equipment, and allowing them to show, not hide their bodies. A complaint from one of the girls I work with, which was far from unusual, was: 'My mum won't let me wear skirts. She says I should hide my legs because they're ugly, but I don't want to!' Another was unhappy because: 'All my sisters are allowed to have long hair, except me. It doesn't make sense.' I can vouch for the fact that it didn't make sense. A third, who uses calipers and crutches, was fed up with being denied the chance to go out and choose her own shoes. I am thrilled that each girl has been able to assert herself well enough to have overcome these obstacles to their growing independence and self-esteem.

Another problem has proved harder to solve, and it relates closely both to being allowed to grow up, and to building self-confidence and life skills, and therefore breaking down isolation. This is the issue of letting our children go out on their own. Now I am not suggesting any blanket rules – apart from anything else it will never be an option for some of our children, though it may be possible to let them be taken out by their peers during their teenage years. Nor am I suggesting that there may not be a need for quite lengthy training – there may. The point is that we would do well to aim for this, because there are few things more galling to most teenagers than to be unable to be seen in public unless one is hanging on a parent's arm.

Naturally, what makes it so hard for us to take this on board is knowing how dangerous the world out there can be, and the natural desire to see that our children come to no harm. But in fact, as with non-disabled teenagers, if we keep them at home or permanently by our sides, they will never learn, and never become streetwise. As we have seen, the more knowledge our disabled children have, the better protected they become.

To this end, there are some courses on personal safety run specifically for disabled young people by the Suzy Lamplugh Trust (see Resources section). But for some of us the issues are much more basic than that. We can feel that our children could never manage a bus ride alone, or would be cheated by shop-keepers into parting with their money for rubbish. The truth is that there are usually ways of teaching skills for dealing with these situations and that most schools are willing and able to help if approached. Indeed it may be the school initiating the idea and it needs all the support we can give, despite the fact we might be quaking in our boots!

I remember trying to mediate between a family with a teenage girl with learning difficulties and the school on just such an issue. The school had arranged a work placement for the girl, which would require her to use a bus on her own, and the family were forcefully blocking it. The teacher in question believed that the family just had no faith in their daughter and were not prepared to give her a chance, and to some extent I thought she was right. But it *was* more complex than that. The family were Bangladeshi and this was the East End of London. They claimed that they would have let her go to another shop in a different area, but that the area around the shop the school had chosen was a focus for racial attacks. The school, on the other hand, had no links with the shops in the area the family said they were happy about, and therefore no way of arranging a placement there. I honestly suspect it was six of one and half a dozen of the other. It seemed to me that had the school used an interpreter, and made better links with the family from the start, this episode might have been avoided.

This may appear to be straying from the area of sexual development, but it isn't. Part of our being able to see ourselves as women or men, as opposed to girls or boys, lies in the roles we adopt. If we can have faith in ourselves as real women or men in terms of roles, it gives us more chance of believing in our sexuality. If we don't believe in that we can neither nurture it nor guard it. This does not mean that I think that anyone should adhere to social prescriptions or stereotypes about 'real' men or women, I don't think a boy or man must be macho to be a real boy or man, for instance. The whole issue centres around whether or not we are prepared to let our children 'grow up' and take their rightful place in the world as adults. It is about not getting in the way of their expressed desires to pursue whatever paths they want to follow.

Disabled young people need a sense that we, as parents, are able to contemplate their sexuality and their need for sexual exploration and, in most cases, relationships. It is vital that we don't beat down signs of developing sexuality, whatever our feelings. Too many young disabled people find themselves being told quite explicitly 'I don't know why you're bothering, who's going to look at you?' Remember that we are not the only people giving our children messages about themselves. I recall, with triumph, the look on my arch-enemy's face when she saw me with my first boyfriend. He was gorgeous and six feet tall! Written across her forehead were the words 'How is it possible!'

Trying out make-up and hairstyles, fashions and music are our given right, all part of our healthy sexual development. If our children can't just go out and do it for themselves, we could help them. We should treat shopping with a disabled teenager just as we treat shopping with any teenager– a balancing act between our own feelings towards the latest outrageous fashion and our desire to encourage their taste and freedom of choice. Sure enough we, and they, might have to face up to the censorship of others, but then that is a normal aspect of parenthood. If we believe in ourselves and our children, that's a fight we will be prepared to take on.

Of course, being open to our child's sexual development means accepting their sexuality, even if it differs from our own. The 'asexual' stereotype tends to obscure the fact that there are gay and lesbian, as well as heterosexual, disabled people and, without exception, they will be much more psychologically healthy if they are allowed to celebrate their sexuality openly. There are organisations specifically for disabled gays and lesbians and they can provide invaluable support to a young person who is finding their way.

Perhaps the most problematic issue, which may not surface until quite late on, is that of sexual stimulation for young people who cannot masturbate for themselves. Here I have to say I don't know a safe answer before the legal age for consenting sex, unless the young person is able to manage aids such as vibrators for themselves. Apart from anything else, if a child has never been able to 'play with themselves' it is unlikely that they would require or request to be masturbated. And it is not safe for us to conclude for the child that they need it, however normal such experimentation may be. One colleague of mine reports five cases in which perpetrators of abuse have used the excuse that they were teaching the child to masturbate. I believe the only safe thing to do is to wait until a young person expresses an interest or desire and at the very least a) has passed the legal age of consent and b) can communicate Yes and No and understand basic questions.

I am in agreement with some of my colleagues that a clear guideline is that no one in a caring role should also be involved in sexual stimulation. The issue of boundaries is vital here. For instance, a carer can put a young person in such a position that they could then explore their bodies by themselves, or masturbate, but the carer should have no part in that.

There is an opinion, practised in the Netherlands, that after the age of consent disabled people should have access to all aspects of the sex industry, from prostitution to pornography, since that is the right of non-disabled people. I have great difficulty with that because on the one hand, I believe in equal rights for disabled people and on the other, much of the sex industry is rooted in child abuse.

It is probably already apparent that we may have as much work to do on ourselves as on our children! It should be emphasised, then, that we should work through our own attitudes first, dealing with our sticking points with trusted friends or partners, so that we have every chance of being an excellent resource for our children.

Our sexuality is something we have a right to enjoy and celebrate. The more we can do so, the more sure we become of what we do and don't want. The worse we feel about our sexuality, the more desperate we can become for sexual overtures, and the more vulnerable we are to abuse. Young people with intentional communication, who have vocabulary for private parts of their body, and are comfortable using these, are less likely to allow themselves to be exploited by their peers.

Whilst we should never expect our children to protect themselves, we can build protective layers around them.

Section Two
Our Children in the Hands of
Professionals and Institutions

Chapter Five

Pots of Professionals

Doctors, consultants, nurses, physiotherapists, occupational therapists, health visitors, peripatetic teachers, support teachers, educational psychologists, specialist social workers, residential social workers, care managers, family link workers, transport drivers, transport assistants, specialist youth workers . . .

It is natural for us to want any advice and assistance we can get for our children. Fortunately *and* unfortunately there are a whole host of professionals out there who have, or think they have, something useful to contribute.

For many years it was relatively easy to get referrals to a wide range of professionals. However, as state provision was constantly hacked back in the drive to privatise, it became more and more problematic for an increasing number of people. It is also true that those of us who are not white and British, and have working-class accents have often had more difficulty in accessing help due to such factors as racism and classism. In other words, the fewer the resources, the more ways the system must find of screening out requests for help.

I remember the mother of a young woman with profound learning difficulties and physical impairments explaining to me how it was that she had never had equipment to help with such tasks as bathing. She was Turkish and said, 'I ring up, but as soon as they hear my accent, that's it!' Unable to gain access to social workers, she asked the caretaker of her block of flats for advice, and was promptly told that she was not eligible for any benefits! The less contact we have with professional circles, the easier it is for other people to persuade us that we are not entitled to any help from those quarters.

Most of us will probably have encountered a large and varied range of professionals, some of whom will have been wonderfully supportive, and some who will have been downright destructive. Some disability activists have pointed out that society first makes life impossible for us, and then pays fat wages to a huge range of people to patch up, but never change, the ensuing problems.[1] This is in part true, that some people's jobs would not exist but for the oppression of disabled people, but it is also true that we would still need the services of at least some of the people listed above, even in an ideal world. So, we would not need transport workers if all public transport were fully accessible to people with all and any impairments, but we would still need speech and language therapists to perform at least a good proportion of their work.

In terms of protecting our children, this plethora of professionals has both advantages and disadvantages. The main advantage is that one, or a number of these people may be able to spot signs and indicators of abuse if no one else has. But also, at the preventative level, they may be helping our children to develop in such a way as to make them less vulnerable to abuse. Thus a child who is being given equipment to allow them to take care of their own toileting needs is being helped to achieve independence in a setting often used by perpetrators of abuse. Or a speech and language therapist who is helping a child use a communication system is making it easier for a child to 'tell' and this makes them a less attractive proposition for an abuser.

However, there are also two main disadvantages of our children being dealt with by all these different people. The first is that, of course, there are perpetrators amongst any and every profession. So the more professionals our children are left alone with, the more they are at risk. This is a very uncomfortable fact for parents, because we need to be able to trust the people to whom we turn for help. I certainly do not suggest that we treat every professional with suspicion, but it is vital that we achowledge the risk and deal with it with our eyes open. The second disadvantage is that all these people do not necessarily communicate well with each other, and sometimes each is holding some information which, if it were shared, might be beneficial for the child. For example, a care worker may notice the child developing an interest in some activity, and if this information is shared with the child's school, the school can then capitalise on that new hobby.

It has to be said that there are other disadvantages too. Sometimes a child's life is so full of visits to or by various professionals that there is no space for them to be children, socialising with their family and friends. This can mean, for instance, that their speech is vastly improved, but that they end up with little to talk about. It can distort the lives of the parents and the whole family too. Also, it can be damaging to a child's self-esteem to perceive themselves as being so absolutely dependent on so many adults. Disabled young people involved in the

Council for Disabled children's focus group were eloquent about some of these problems.

> I get tired of all those people, it's assessment all the time. Sometimes they ask me what I think, but not all the time.
>
> I wish we didn't have to see so many people, I can't even remember your names. Sometimes they talk to each other not me!
>
> I think they are getting better. They know about children's rights – well, sort of. But I wish they knew more about disability, I mean, it's sort of embarrassing to have to explain yourself.
>
> It would be much better if we had lists of all the people we saw and who they are. Like a family tree . . . then we'd know where we were.

It can therefore be important to advocate for our children, insisting on fewer appointments with professionals, and perhaps suggesting that these people co-ordinate with each other, so that our child has some chance of living a child's life.

Also, children are rarely asked what kind of help they would most value at a particular time. For example, I remember working with a bright young boy in Kenya. He had cerebral palsy and was also profoundly deaf. The professionals deemed it most important to get him walking, but I observed that he was intelligent and extremely frustrated at his limited communication skills. So I began to teach him some sign language and he gobbled it up. He couldn't get enough of our signing lessons and learnt almost as many signs as I could teach him in any one session. In contrast he bitterly resisted any attempt to put him in calipers and get him walking. So, fair enough, it wasn't possible to ask him 'Which is most important for you right now, walking or talking?', but by trying a bit of both, his choice was plain to see.

We do need to respect these choices and not let professionals frighten us into trying to do everything at once. I'm quite sure that once that child was communicating confidently he might have become more interested in walking and put in the effort required. All of us make these choices about what we prioritise at any given time. During one period of my life, for example, I was interested in doing minor car maintenance for myself; right now I can't think of many things lower on my priority list! So why can't we let children decide, and honour their priorities? Of course there will be a few exceptions, where particular exercises or treatments might be urgent, but the truth is that all professionals are bound to think that what they have to offer is the most important. Again, *we* are the only ones with the whole picture, and our children need to retain some sense of control over their lives, as well as their bodies.

Professionals outside our homes
Child Protection professionals

There are various specific problems related to child protection professionals and their attitudes to or knowledge of protecting disabled children. The most profound and most disheartening attitude is that exemplified by a Director of Social Services after he had given a talk about the policies and procedures for child protection that he had put in place in his local authority. As he had not mentioned disabled children at all, he was asked, 'What about the disabled children?' To which he replied, 'Let me deal with the normal children first.' Never was there a clearer admission of how little disabled children are valued. Three years on from this man's retort, some local authorities *still* have not got any policies and procedures in place. Some have the odd line here and there, but give little or no direction or support to the workers. Very few local authorities have included enough detail. Why?

One reason, it has to be said, is that there are some awful professional ideas which essentially blame disabled children for their own abuse, particularly physical abuse. Thus some child protection workers and writers discuss confidently 'abuse provoking characteristics in disabled children'. This concept is mostly applied to children with behaviour that is very difficult to manage, but is also applied to children whose conditions make great demands on their carers. This concept is totally unacceptable to me and to many others. Whatever the nature of a child's behaviour, the adult can *always* choose to leave the room, get help, or, if necessary, let out a yell of frustration, rather than abuse. Victim blaming is vicious and directs our attention in all the wrong places. But it provides an easy way out, which, unhappily, overstretched professionals may be all too happy to take.

To some extent it is pure ignorance. To some extent it is professional neglect. It is not unrelated to the desperate staffing levels to which Social Services around the country have been reduced. It is also symptomatic of something many parents and foster parents have pointed out to me: there are still a lot of social workers out there who are terrified of disabled children.

Just recently I was training foster parents for one local authority and suggested they ask for as much detail as possible about a child's needs before meeting the child. One woman retorted:

You must be joking! The last child they left with me, the social worker just turns up with the child on the doorstep one night, and says, 'This is X that I told you about' – and that was all she'd told me, her name, and then she ran away! I had no idea what this kid needed and I'd never had a kid with her condition before. But since then I can hardly get the social worker in the same room as her. She looks at her as if she might bite!

There are those of us who are offering training to get workers over this most basic of stumbling blocks, but, of course, we can only respond when we are approached. Some parents and carers have got what it takes, both in terms of time and ability, to help the social worker. But it should not be necessary and most parents have plenty to do without this additional burden.

Once there is a suspicion of abuse, many social workers can not, and do not, put it through the child protection system. They instantly switch to the medical model of disability and bring in occupational therapists and physiotherapists, for example, to deal with the symptoms rather than the cause. Presumably influenced by the myth that nobody would stoop so low, they leave the child unprotected. This is another area in which the service the child gets can depend entirely on the tenacity, eloquence and confidence of the person making the referral. Unfortunately, the latter are often the lowest down the professional hierarchy, with the least confidence and the least job security. So, if ever we make a referral and are dissatisfied with the response, we would do well to turn ourselves into tenacious bulldogs and not let go until we are completely satisfied. Certainly this takes courage. I would always advise workers to seek support from their managers, and others if necessary.

Disability workers

Here I include not just the paramedical professionals, but also those who deliver respite care, youth or play workers and school support workers. They too are sometimes unwilling to admit that disabled children might be abused. Often this is because the perpetrator is a colleague. Perhaps they are friends. Perhaps the perpetrator has been their mentor at work, or the one who keeps everyone else's spirits up. The perpetrator may be the one with the most experience. The worst scenario is that they are the one with the most power. Whatever the reason, it is not hard to understand why workers often stand up for each other, especially when the evidence is subtle or difficult to interpret. It must be extremely difficult to contemplate the possibility that a trusted colleague might abuse children.

But I have heard too many stories like the one a mother told me recently.

> G had terrible marks down his back. I asked at the home [where G lives] and no one seemed to know anything about it. When I took G to the doctor, he said it looked as though my son had been dragged down a brick wall. But I never got to the bottom of it.

This leaves many disturbing questions:

- Why didn't anyone at the home alert this mother to the abrasions?
- Why didn't the doctor make a child protection referral?
- Why hadn't the mother been given a clear set of instructions from the home and/or the social worker as to what to do in the event of signs and indicators of abuse?
- Why didn't the home initiate its own investigation and/or ask Social Services to investigate?

Institutions should have clear policy and procedures which they convey to children as far as possible and which are certainly conveyed to all parents, in writing. It is wise to ask each institution at which we leave our child to give us copies of these. The likelihood is that they won't have them, but asking may jolt the powers that be into action.

Certainly, one way that disability workers often throw social workers off the scent (and, it has to be said, so do abusing parents), is by throwing at them their great experience of disabled children in general and 'this child' in particular. A social worker who is unsure of themselves in relation to disability is easily undermined by someone who says, 'You don't know these children/this child. I do. I've worked/lived with them for twenty years. I'm telling you there is nothing to worry about.'

Now sometimes disability workers throw their weight about in this way, not because they have something to hide, but precisely because they are so powerless professionally – often underpaid and undervalued. This means that it is in parents' interests to show that they value good workers, by telling not only the particular worker how pleased they are, but also by telling that person's boss. Just as it is dangerous to have disempowered children, it is problematic to have disempowered staff.

On another training course, after a discussion about what it means to include disabled children in play settings, a play worker ventured to voice her concern about the way a support worker was behaving. She started this way:

> This woman, she really knows her stuff and she's done wonders for T, but she always keeps the rest of us away from T, especially the other children, saying that it would distract her from learning the skills she's teaching T. She really is an expert, but . . .

This young woman needed the rest of the afternoon and the intervention of a manager on the course, backing me up, to be reassured that her concern was a serious and well-founded one, and that it was irrelevant if this worker had ten degrees and thirty years' experience. It is a matter of grave concern when a worker isolates a child in this way. One has to ask what is in it for the worker to make the child so absolutely dependent on her. Also, an isolated child is not a child who can tell anyone if something bad is happening to them.

What is worrying is that people like this young woman feel that unless they have facts and figures, or equal years of experience to back up their concerns, they must keep quiet. Gut feelings *are* important. It doesn't matter if someone else has to turn those feelings into accurate detail; they really must be shared and chased up persistently. The truth is that a worker who is truly knowledgeable, and experienced, and respectful of a child's rights, will always listen respectfully to other people's concerns. This seems to me to be the crux of the matter for many parents seeking to protect their children. We need to have the confidence or simply the audacity to shout when we are concerned, even if we seem to be the least educated or experienced person involved.

Protection strategies

In general then, there are a number of things we can do to protect our children in relation to these professionals who see our children out of the home, and sometimes in our absence.

The first is to assert our right to a full and clear explanation as to the value of any new professional input. We can check that no other professional already dealing with our child could possibly do what the new person is supposed to do (sometimes one set of exercises can get incorporated into another, for instance). This means that we are also asserting our right to refuse professional input. It has to be said that this takes great self-confidence and a good understanding of the whole picture, but the latter is what most professionals exactly lack.

It is also crucial that we listen to what our child has to say about any particular professional and take seriously any unhappiness or unease that they express. If our child uses an informal system of non-verbal communication, we can observe how they appear before and after appointments. Their behaviour will tell us quite a lot about how happy or unhappy they are with a particular professional. If our child expresses any unhappiness or fear, this needs following up. Is it the person or the procedure, or perhaps both? Could either or both be altered? Most procedures do not have to be unpleasant or painful, and when they truly do, children can usually tell the difference between useful pain (that is, for example, stretching a muscle), and needless pain. And of course there is no need for any professional to be unpleasant!

Professionals in our homes

Having people help you in your own home is most definitely a burden as well as a blessing, and parents have to work very hard to get the balance right for their children as well as for themselves. Even when we are at home with our children, if there are a number of care workers coming in to give assistance it raises child protection issues. Perhaps the most difficult situation arises when we need a great deal of help over a long period. Then, no matter how well we may get on with our helpers, we and our children face repeated losses and new adjustments, as people leave in search of better paid employment, work closer to home, and other such considerations. It becomes painful watching children struggling to come to terms with the loss of the last worker and the adjustments necessary for the new one. The real danger is that they get a message that they must accept all new adults who come into their lives. Few aspects of my need for help have worried me more.

New workers

It is really important to make new helpers take their time getting to know a child. Too many think that the way to demonstrate how good they are with children is to swoop on them instantly with cries of delight, and hug them and hold them before the child has even had a good look, or listen, or feel of the person. This is truly dangerous for the child because if this becomes a repeated experience, the child is getting the message that they are public property.

I learnt to tell each new person that I wanted them just to sit and talk first, and let the children get used to them before touching. Whilst we talked I would be observing how they behaved with the children. Were they interested, or did they just start going on about the job? Did they say anything complimentary about the children? Or did they simply commiserate with me about how much hard work it must be? Did they make themselves accessible to the children physically, by how they talked, or did they make themselves distant? Did they accept the children as they were, or did they want them to be smiling and demonstrating an immediate liking for the person?

I had to decide to be very tough and not accept people whose behaviour wasn't up to scratch, because I soon learnt to regret any time I didn't trust my gut feelings about someone. Equally, after one awful incident (see page 112) I decided that I would not allow any new worker to give intimate care to my children until I had seen that the girls were comfortable and relaxed with them, and certainly not until they had been there at least a day.

I also decided to be up front about the things that were important to me concerning the care of the children as quickly as possible. It wasn't always easy because there tended to be a string of demands that needed attending to, often from the moment the worker stepped through the door, but I had to try. I would say, for example, that I didn't leave them to cry but tried to work out what the message was, and that I never tried to stop them crying. I also made it clear that what I wanted was teamwork. In other words, I was not turning my children over to them wholesale.

For all parents of disabled children, then, it is very important to have a clear idea of your expectations, and to commmunicate these to each new worker in an effective way.

Established workers

There is a lot to be learnt on both sides. It is vital to set up high expectations about the worker communicating with us about our children, and we must prioritise communicating with them. My best helper was a quiet and shy woman, who very slowly came to trust me enough to share anything about herself. But from the beginning she would tell me anything she thought I should know about the children, and always showed a real interest in them. First thing in the morning she would greet me and then take time greeting the children. Then I would tell her anything of concern or interest that had happened during the night. As the day progressed she would tell me anything she noticed, from a new development, to rashes, to clothes being too tight. I learnt a great deal from her and often require other workers to do some tasks as she did. For instance, when she laid the girls down to change a nappy she would then take a few moments making eye contact and talking to the girls before she began to remove clothing. This eased the process enormously and meant there was no struggle at all.

But there are enormous dilemmas as one gets to know a worker. What do we insist they do our way, and what do we let them do theirs? It's no good requiring them to do everything our way because they are not us and it is too much of a strain (it is also insulting to suggest that their ways are never good enough). On the other hand, if they do everything their way, the children might begin to feel like theirs, not ours, and the worker may come to disrespect us. The child might be left wondering who is the parent!

So it is helpful to talk to others and decide what we will insist on, and where we can give some leeway. This is particularly true in relation to intimate care. Just as Ruth Marchant and I have pointed out the need for institutions to have policy and procedure around intimate care, so it is also a good idea for parents.[2] We can tell any worker or groups of workers who will provide intimate care how we want it done. This ensures as much continuity as possible for the child and gives everyone a sense of security. If a worker raises objections, it is wise to listen well. Are they objecting because they have a better suggestion, or are they rubbishing ours? The former is worth learning from and the latter distinctly worrying.

One other tip is that I learnt to enquire whether workers had children of their own and to express an interest. Some workers expressed attitudes towards their own children that left me convinced that they would need to be watched quite carefully.

One can't hover over workers' shoulders all the time. On the other hand, we should be able to intervene if something goes wrong. I have been unable to forgive myself for failing to prevent something that traumatised one of my girls and has left her still struggling with toileting problems. A new helper had arrived. This woman was so awful that within a couple of hours I rang the agency and asked for a replacement. But it was impossible for me to send her out of the door before the replacement came because I physically couldn't manage alone. When the replacement came, Ms Dreadful was in the process of changing one of the girls' nappy. She was cleaning the girl's bottom and the replacement was looking on, so there was not much room for me. But my daughter began to cry bitterly and I managed to see that this woman was scrubbing away at her bottom with dry cotton wool. For whatever reason (I can think of several but they now feel like inadequate excuses), instead of sending her away that instant, I just asked rather feebly whether she couldn't wet the cotton wool. She didn't and eventually I said, 'That's enough,' and picked up my screaming and trembling daughter and had to comfort her for a very long time. But the damage was done.

This illustrates the dilemmas we can find ourselves in and, more importantly, the dilemmas in which our disabled children find themselves. My dependency on this woman's help meant I couldn't throw her out immediately. So it is for disabled children. Their dependency on people makes it hard for them even to imagine they have a right to ask for change, or complain, let alone do anything about it. In other words, if I as an adult in that situation felt powerless, how much more powerless must our children feel?

Workers supporting us in the home

Some of us, especially if we are disabled ourselves, have people helping us at home who are not there to provide child care, but are there to help *us* – most commonly with housework such as cleaning. Obviously we have fewer concerns about such people because their contact with our children is less direct, but there are issues to be addressed nevertheless. These people do still have access to the children and can influence them. It is now commonly accepted that people working in the homes of others, especially where there are children, should not smoke. Equally, it is important to me that if one of my children cries she should not be told anything along the lines of 'Come on now, stop that noise.'

Again, however, there is the simple fact of access and need; perpetrators can – and do – play on one's needs to increase their access, by making themselves so trusted that we are tempted to blur the boundaries of what we allow, or invite them to do. Also, we still have the same problems with frequent changes in personnel. It is really not a safe message to be giving out to the children if we have a succession of different people in our homes. We want the greatest continuity possible, but the more help we need, the further this aim seems to vanish into thin air.

This is especially true for single parents, disabled or not. They have a far greater need for help, even if only in terms of child care, and are very vulnerable because of their need. There is no doubt that poor provision of services can put single parents in an impossible position and thereby increases the likelihood of children being left in unsatisfactory or even downright dangerous circumstances. Single parents of disabled children are sometimes the most socially isolated of all – even if they have a lot of contact with professionals – and we should all take responsibility for breaking down that isolation in any way we can.

With so much going on, then, how can we keep a watchful eye on the whole picture?

Reviews

Reviews of our child's progress should be times when we, and all the professionals involved in our child's life, can share information and where we should be able to get support. All too often, unfortunately, parents find themselves sitting listening to the views, and worse still the decisions, of others, with hardly a thought being given to consulting either the parents or the child. We must not accept this type of situation. Professionals are very good at taking over. They may not mean to, but in the effort to introduce their knowledge and expertise to the situation (and sometimes to impress their colleagues), they can be domineering and disrespectful. If we don't demand respect, our child may not get it either!

It is often true that parents and carers who really stick up for the rights of their children get labelled as troublemakers. We have to learn to be proud of this label, rather than being daunted by it. Perhaps this is why one group of parents got together and called themselves Parents with Attitude! They produced a booklet forcefully arguing for inclusive education for their children.[3] Certainly it is helpful to talk to other parents in similar positions and some local authorities do actively promote this. If we are finding it difficult to meet other parents, being persistent with all the professionals we have to deal with will eventually provide contacts.

If we do send our child for out-of-home respite care in an institution – not honestly something I recommend, far better that *we* get respite and leave our child in a familiar setting – then we could try to arrange it for when the child's best known or best liked workers are on duty. At least we could ask what the institution does to minimise the number of carers, and request to see their Intimate Care and Child Protection policy and procedures. In itself this sends a message that this child is not to be messed with and again might prompt some institutional development.

This chapter is not intended to be over-critical of professionals. Many are working very actively to improve matters for our children, and many do welcome close contact and full discussion with parents and carers. Rather I want to point out the pivotal role we can play in helping professionals and institutions to care constructively for our children.

Overall we need to keep in mind our child's rights to: a childhood; absolute approval as they are; consultation about what is to happen and observation of how they are reacting to any intervention.

Chapter Six

Medical Intervention

My own feeling is that this is one of the trickiest areas for parents because it is full of dilemmas, and because many of the decisions that must be made are complex and may have life-long implications for our children. I went through absolute agony deciding whether or not to let my children have vaccinations. I did, and regretted it because they immediately developed eczema, but I'm fairly sure that I would *also* have regretted deciding not to, because of the level of anxiety it would probaby have produced in me! So it is clear that there are no easy answers, and many grey areas.

Why is medical intervention such an issue? Well, mainly because the medical model of disability has created a sort of general acceptance that medical intervention in the lives of disabled children must be necessary, and must be 'a good thing'. The reality of disability being a socially constructed affair, with impairment as a very different issue, cautions us to think twice about this. We have to ask ourselves, '*What* exactly are we seeking to change and *why*?' The other truly difficult thing for us as parents is that these questions throw us up against our own attitudes fairly forcefully. Without acknowledging these and dealing with them, we and our children are in quite a vulnerable position. Obviously each person will have a different way of confronting their own attitudes and overcoming any difficult or disconcerting feelings. Some of us may seek a professional counsellor, others know that our family and friends can help us to a more positive position. What counts is trying to end up with the most *respectful* position in relation to our children.

The best approach to medical intervention is to develop certain principles on which to base our decisions, rather than being blown about by the welter of different opinions we will encounter.

Resisting the tyranny of the god 'normality'

The principle my parents went by and which I acquired, is that what matters most is being able to get on with your life, feeling good about yourself. I have a very short left leg and until I was about 11, had worn either a big raise called a patten, or a caliper. But then the doctors persuaded my parents that as a teenager I would want to look more 'normal', especially at parties or dances, and so I was offered an artificial leg. I seem to remember that my parents put no pressure on me whatsoever to wear it and it spent most of its time sticking out between two cupboards in my bedroom, frightening people. But I did wear it sometimes and discovered the cost of deception! Where I had previously only had to deal with stares, I was now fielding questions like 'Have you fallen off a bike?' or 'Have you sprained your ankle?' as people noticed my limp and the apparent swelling at the ankle where my toes fitted in. I was rapidly becoming disillusioned and when I found a boyfriend who couldn't care less whether or not I wore it, I abandoned it with some relief. So I'm glad I learnt that it was easier if people could see what the problem was, more or less, and that my parents made decisions that allowed me to learn in this way. But, of course, this was something that could be worn or cast off, so the implications were not at all grave, unlike many operations and procedures.

There is one other thing to note here. Whilst it is true that my own artificial limb was a ghastly salmon colour and had to be covered by three stockings, with two on the other leg to get some semblance of match in colour, the situation was far worse for black people, as no effort was made at all to get the colour right for them. Although these pigments have now been developed, families may still find themselves having to be assertive about getting the limb colour right.

Listening to many other disabled people, however, I get the same message. Pretence is not only harder to deal with psychologically, but it is damaging to the self-esteem. If I am only acceptable via pretence it means I am not acceptable as I am. Also, most of us find excellent ways of coping without pretence. We can find it much easier using methods we have devised ourselves to deal with everyday tasks, or involving straightforward but unglamorous equipment, than struggling with artificial body parts. There's a delightful story about a small girl who so hated her artificial arm that she would secrete it in her father's deep coat pocket and he would find it there when he reached in for his lunch at work!

In essence then, given that there is no such thing as a normal human being anyway, operations, equipment or procedures designed purely to make children seem more 'normal' in some way are inherently insulting. They are also dangerous. Parents, and children, can feel compelled to seek out more and more (often expensive) intervention, all in the name of this god normality. It can bankrupt parents, or force them into making their children charity cases as they seek treatment abroad, perhaps, and deprive the child of any shred of self-esteem or of any normal childhood experiences. This, although perhaps done with the best of intentions, is an essentially abusive practice. Good practitioners make a distinction between trying to make the child more normal, and trying to create more normal function in some part of their bodies. It is impossible to object, for instance, to exercises designed to strengthen a weak limb so that it can function more normally. But not everything is this straightforward.

One of the big things likely to get in the way of our making rational assessments is *our own* need to feel normal, or our worries about how other people will see and treat us, as well as our children. Parents can be tempted to consider that they want such and such for their child for the child's sake when actually the parent is the one seeking to avoid embarrassment or shame. This is neither unexpected nor something to feel guilty about because society fails to give parents the emotional support we need. However, if we do uncover these feelings in ourselves, we need to work through them with someone we trust, otherwise we can sacrifice our children for our own needs. It is worth remembering that children who feel good about themselves can help us enormously. They can often show us the way to deal with the insults and insensitivities of others.

The cruelty of other children?

One other reason often quoted by parents for accepting operations designed to make their children look more 'normal', is so that they don't have to withstand the cruel jibes and behaviour of other children. I think this is a real slur on children. In my own experience, by far the worst and most stupid remarks and behaviour have always come from adults. This is *not* to suggest that children are never cruel, they sometimes are. But then that is often because others are wielding power over them and they are looking for someone weaker than themselves so that they too can wield some power. In this situation, the greatest weapon a disabled child has is complete belief in themselves and their inherent goodness. Then they can deal with difficult children with humour, grace, or just plain sense.

I recall a story my mother told me of coming down the library steps and being stared at by a boy on the pavement. I drew myself up to my full four foot, looked him in the eye and asked haughtily, 'Hasn't your mother taught you not to stare?' Sure enough there are more painful behaviours to deal with. The girls I work with often face taunts of 'spastic, spastic' and are working hard at feeling good enough about themselves in order to deal with it effectively. The children most likely to be bullied and teased are the ones who feel worst about themselves, not the ones with the most unusual appearance. Many appallingly bullied children would melt into any crowd in terms of their appearance, and many children with obvious impairments are very popular and are supported and defended by their classmates.

Moreover, if children can easily be swung towards cruelty it is also true that it does not come naturally and that they can be steered away from it. So it is up to the professionals who look after our children to spot any problem behaviour and to encourage children towards a more healthy attitude to their peers.

What does this mean in terms of medical intervention? It means that our most important goal is helping our children feel good about themselves exactly as they are. In that kind of an atmosphere, a child is in a good position to decide whether or not they want medical intervention, because they know that the consideration is a physical one, not social.

Costs versus benefits

Decisions are inevitably complex, and we need tools to help us. Assessing on balance whether it will cost our child more or benefit them more is one such tool. Doctors are not renowned for assessing the costs to children as well as the benefits of what they propose. They can see the child as a body, rather than a person with a life to lead. Operations are all very well, but our children are removed from the family for them, they often involve considerable pain, sometimes over a very long period and they remove children from their education and their friends. Also most disabled children have to undergo more than one operation. Although most hospitals attempt to offer education to children in for a long stay, it just won't be the same as schooling, not least because the pattern of the day is completely different.

In considering this cost/benefit analysis approach, I remember my reaction to a couple of promotional videos I watched when training people about working with disabled children in developing countries. One was promoting a fairly standard application of the principles of Community Based Rehabilitation – people from a local community being trained to give advice and assistance to families of disabled children, at home or in a local venue. The idea arose because in many developing countries hospital provision is inaccessible to parents of disabled children because it is far away and they cannot afford the transport, let alone medical fees.

Anyway, in this video we saw disabled children who had been kitted out with crutches and calipers made from local resources, struggling along grimly, but with determination. Parents were obviously delighted. In complete contrast was a video which was basically a fundraising effort for an institution in India run along the Ghandian principles of self-help and simplicity.

In this second video, there was not a crutch, caliper or wheelchair in sight. Children hopped, crawled and scuttled, playing football, planting crops, attending the local school via a journey by bullock-cart, and running a printing press. These children absolutely radiated joy and pride in themselves. The image that will stay with me forever, perhaps because I hopped so much as a child myself, is that of a small boy who had obviously had an amputation, hopping speedily along a path and then stopping and waiting without a trace of impatience for his not so speedy friend who had very tiny legs.

My heart is with the children with no equipment but glorious self-esteem. My head says, 'Ah, but they may pay for it in later life as muscles tighten and tendons shorten, in the absence of equipment and operations.' Clearly there is no right or wrong here, but if our focus is on child protection we must never lose sight of the importance of self-esteem as a protective cloak.

It is also worth pointing out here that whilst there are now quite a few companies making specialist equipment, there may be more that we can do for ourselves than we might at first think. Lessening our dependency on professionals can be very important for our children in terms of their emotional well-being, and for us in terms of financial cost. An organisation called People Potential (see Resources list) can help us to design and make equipment. This is also another opportunity for us to involve our children, and if they have had a hand in saying what they want, they are more likely to think positively about a particular piece of equipment.

Our children in hospital

It is important to bear in mind the fact that any operation will require our children to stay in hospital, perhaps for a long period. This of course raises the question of our child's vulnerability to abuse when in the hands of strangers. Whether it is nurses, doctors, porters, physiotherapists or 'domestics', I have heard far too many stories of hospital-based abuse. Hospitals are safer than they used to be, because parents can now often stay by their child's side at night, but most of us have other children and other commitments that mean we can't be there throughout the child's stay. Also children are at their most vulnerable both physically and emotionally when in hospital and it is not always possible to screen out perpetrators. On the other hand, any institution serving children is obliged to run police checks on new recruits before giving them a contract. Unfortunately this provides little protection for the following reasons:

- The police check only uncovers those with previous convictions for offences aainst children. This is only a tiny percentage of all perpetrators since most go either undetected or unconvicted.
- Personnel departments may or may not also check Department of Health and Education lists of those dismissed for gross misconduct.
- Most if not all hospitals now rely heavily on agency staff. Agencies say that they run police checks, but in reality many do not bother because of the length of time it takes.
- It is vital to remember that abusive practice covers many aspects of human behaviour, and of course it is not possible to run a police check on all kinds of abusive practice.
- People like hospital porters may have had no screening at all because, to the best of my knowledge, they are employed to work anywhere in the hospital, not specifically with children.

Pain

Children cope with pain in different ways to adults. All parents will recognise that children in pain tend to sleep a lot. Perhaps this is one reason for the very strange idea, apparently long held by doctors, that children experience less pain than adults and therefore need less pain relief. Research at Great Ormond Street Hospital for Children a couple of years ago uncovered the fact that, allowing for weight differences, doctors were giving children 17 times *less* pain relief than adults! Children at that hospital can now largely determine for themselves when they need relief. But some operations can lead to a lifetime of pain, and children, and usually their parents as well, are not warned of this. Friends of mine testify to the terrible pain experienced by children who have undergone leg lengthening operations; pain that wore off only a little as the years passed.

It is therefore not surprising if doctors make no mention of pain as a significant aspect of operations or procedures which *should* be taken into account in a cost/benefit analysis. We also need to be aware of how frightening it can be for children to hear or witness other children in pain. Obviously one wouldn't use this as the sole reason for refusing treatment, but it should be considered and acknowledged. Adults have more information with which to assess whether someone's distress might have been avoidable, or might be due to mistreatment by the staff. Children, particularly young children, may not have this capacity.

It is also true that we should never settle for any equipment, exercise or procedure that causes our children distress or injury. Distress is *not* the same thing as pain. Most children can tell the difference between a pain that is part of a healing process, and one that is damaging, particularly if we have fully explained what is being done. Children tend to accept pain that they understand and that they sense is healing, but if they cry bitterly each time a particular thing is tried, we should really look at what we are doing carefully. Is the goal right? Could it be achieved another way? We can find ourselves accepting that our children must put up with something just because a professional says so. That is really not good enough and our children need us to advocate on their behalf.

Some important questions

On behalf of the children, then, we parents could first ask ourselves some questions:

- Why am I interested in this operation, equipment or procedure?
- What is it I am wanting for my child?
- Is it just some dream-like normality?
- What do I expect my child to gain?
- What do I expect my child to lose?
- What do I expect our family to gain and lose?

Then there are the questions we could put to doctors and any associated professionals like physiotherapists or speech therapists:

- What do you expect my child to gain?
- How long might it take?
- How much pain might my child go through and how long for?
- How many out-patient appointments might follow – with how many different professionals?
- How much medication is involved, and how long for?
- What are the possible side-effects?
- How do you safeguard children against abuse?
- What is the probability of success?

This process can be much harder for families who do not have English as a first language. It is hard enough for most of us to rally our own assertiveness to be able to question professionals in this way, but when families fear racism, on the one hand, and may have difficulty getting interpreters on the other, it can be nigh on impossible. It is the responsibility of the Health Service to provide interpreters to facilitate this process. This is absolutely critical for the child, for if their parents are feeling nervous in the hospital and unsure of what is going to happen next or why, how much more nervous might the child feel?

No one can be sure how accurate the answers might be. Still, we have a better chance of making wise decisions if we have asked these questions and assessed the answers.

Consulting the child

Doctors are not renowned for respectful treatment of their patients. Although practices are improving, when doctors treat disabled children as objects rather than humans it is not only degrading in itself, it also opens them up to abuse. As one disabled woman said:

> The medical experiences I had made me very vulnerable to being abused and it just seemed the same as everything else that had been done to me, so I couldn't discriminate . . . there is no way you can say no to what a doctor does to you, they just damn well do it when you're a kid. You don't have any choice at all . . . What the doctors did, they lifted up my night-dress, they poked here and they pushed there without asking me, without doing anything, but in front of a load of other people. It was absolutely no different. I didn't say no to any doctor. To me, the porter was doing absolutely nothing different at all than every doctor or nurse had ever done.[1]

So it is absolutely critical to make our children feel that they *do* have a say in what is going on, that they are not just an object, and they can express their anxiety about any proposed medical intervention. It has to be said that it is not possible to consult all children, and it is not possible to give children choices in all situations. But where it is possible we should. Where it is not, we should at least explain what is going to happen and why, even if we think the child might not understand.

When discussing medical intervention with the child we have to be realistic. I have a stark memory of the time that I stood in front of my surgeon after a major change that meant that with my old equipment, walking had become unbearably painful. He looked at me and asked, 'Do you want the pain, or do you want a new way of walking?' Anxious not to appear stupid, but utterly bewildered about what he meant, I opted for the new way of walking! If, then, we are giving the child a choice, then they will need sound information in a form they can understand. They will also have to know their choice will be honoured. It's no good saying, 'Do you want to have an operation to straighten your spine?' without explaining to the child a great deal of what that means, in terms of the answers to the questions we have already asked the doctor. A child will have no real concept of the implications. And if the child responds in the negative, allowing our own anxieties and desire for the operation to override their answer will make a mockery of the process of consultation.

So, we have to be sure of as many of the facts as we can, and we have to have settled within ourselves that we can live with our children's answers. If we know for a fact that we couldn't cope with our children refusing an operation or treatment, that we are absolutely certain it will go ahead, then we should not pretend to consult them. If we feel that the question is too big for our child with their present state of knowledge and understanding of the world, then we shouldn't ask the question either. In these circumstances, we might consult our children about some other aspect of the proposed treatment. For example, 'We have decided that it is best you have an operation to help you see better, but the doctor says it is not urgent. Would you prefer to have it before the school holidays so that you can go back to school as soon as possible after term starts, or would you prefer to have it after the holidays so you can go away with your brothers and sisters? In other words, we should let the child have some say in the matter even if it is a more minor aspect of the whole issue. The child who has been consulted will feel far more in control of what can be a frightening process, far more respected and far more willing to co-operate with whatever exercises or procedures might be necessary.

More needs to be said, though, about the child we cannot consult because they would not understand the questions, the information, or the meaning of the process. Many people have noted that before you do something it helps to tell the child that you are about to do it. We can give as much or as little information as makes us comfortable; what is important is that this demonstrates a real respect for the child. If they can't understand, they nevertheless have the comfort of your familiar voice, and if you do this as a matter of course, then they may at least come to associate it with something being 'about to happen' so that that 'something' does not take them by surprise too much. If they can understand at all it will help them cope, and sometimes they will be able to do something helpful to assist the process, even if it is merely by relaxing.

You can demand of staff that they do this too, and most are only too willing, because it is actually more natural and human to be talking to someone as you do something to them, than to be silent.

The child needs to know that you are willing to listen to all they want to communicate about their experience in hospital – that you are willing to listen to the pain as well as the things that are fun or interesting. It is also critical that they know that they can tell you anything that has happened that has disturbed or frightened them. Children in hospital can have a very hard time distinguishing legitimate procedures from abuse (not least because doctors so rarely seek permission from children for what they do), and they should not be expected to be able to make that distinction. If, however, they know that you will listen to absolutely everything, there is a chance that you can put an early stop to any abuse or abusive practice that has happened.

In general, whenever we take our children for any professional appointment we should try to find out in advance what is going to happen, and brief our children before they get there, in a way that makes sense to them. This has many advantages. If we find out ourselves what is likely to happen, it helps us be more prepared and therefore relaxed, and that communicates itself to our children. If the children know what to expect they are likely to be less fretful and more co-operative, both with us and with the professionals involved, especially when the procedure is in any way physically or emotionally demanding. Finally, if staff diverge from the path they led you to expect, you have some grounds for challenging them.

Routines

If a child does have a stay in hospital then it is helpful to pass on to staff any routines you adhere to at home, in case they can do them the same way or at the same point in the day. This gives the child some small continuity and breaks down very slightly the sense of having moved into a different world. Hospital staff have a far greater understanding these days of the needs of children and are much better about child centred methods. Nevertheless they can't know things like how your child is normally comforted when they are distressed and telling them in front of the child is helpful to everyone.

Equally, it is important that parents feel able to share with hospital staff any medical or practical routines that have been developed and are successful at home. Sometimes parents feel that staff will automatically know how to do things, forgetting the small details that are personal but make a huge difference. If, for instance, your child must have manual evacuation of the bowels, and you have worked out a successful routine at home, involving when it is done (eg after breakfast) and how (eg with prior massage of the abdomen) it is really helpful for staff and your child for that to be continued in hospital. Sometimes hospital staff overlook asking for these details, not because they think they know it all, but under pressure of time. They usually appreciate any help you can give them about making the child feel 'at home'.

Medical photography

This is one particular area where there has been much abusive practice. You would normally be consulted as the parent or carer of a child, if staff wished to take photographs of your child. Many of us agree on the assumption that if they ask they must have good reason. This is not necessarily the case. They may be asking so that they can build a portfolio of photographic case notes, for publication or teaching purposes. You may feel quite happy about your child being used in this way, but you may not and nor may your child. So always ask the purpose of the photography, consult your child where possible, and feel strong enough to refuse permission.

If you agree to photography, it must be performed in the most respectful manner.

- Children should again be informed of *exactly* what is going to happen (even if their permission could not be sought).
- They should not have to remove any but the most essential clothing and should be introduced to the photographer/s.
- They should have you or someone else they trust close by.
- They should not be kept in uncomfortable positions or surroundings for any length of time.
- They should not have to witness their photographs being passed around students or anyone else.

Medication

Some medication is vital for some of our children; it is life-preserving or life-saving. Some medication is essential in emergency situations. There is no doubt that some of us, and some of our children, have had to learn to live with it.

There is, however, another side to the story and that is a much more disturbing one. People tend to turn to medication much too easily to get rid of disturbed, disturbing or 'challenging' behaviour. I strongly suspect that there are thousands of children, and adults, out there, particularly those with learning difficulties, who have been trying to tell us something for years, but their efforts have been medicated away, because their message was uncomfortable for us to handle.

I am very uneasy, as are many professionals, about one of the latest American medical trends to hit the UK, which is calling hyperactive behaviour Attention Deficit Syndrome. I might not have been quite so uneasy if the preferred treatment were not amphetamines, or 'speed' as it is called on the drugs scene. Of course, there may be some children who have a genuine medical problem, but I am sure that there are also many who are trying to tell us that something has gone badly wrong in their lives and that it needs to be addressed. If these behaviours are 'drugged' out of sight, we are telling the child we are not interested in their story; we are only interested in controlling them. If some of them are trying to tell us about abuse, this is profoundly depressing and disempowering, since abuse is also always about control. An 'easy' child is not necessarily a psychologically healthy one.

Obviously it is simple to sit far away from any particular child and their behaviour and warn against the use of drugs. The truth is I have great sympathy for anyone living with a child who, for example, sleeps little and rushes around with enough energy for four. At the same time I know that if a problem is being buried under drugs, then that problem will try and try forever to make its voice heard, and we could be sentencing the child to a lifetime of drug use. There is a sense in which the use of behaviour altering drugs is one of the greatest ways in which we, as a society or as individuals, exercise power. All I ask is that parents and carers insist that everything else be tried before drugs are resorted to, and that even then, other avenues continue to be sought. It is also important that parents seek not just one but several opinions, possibly from different professionals, before going down this road.

In conclusion

Fundamentally, of course, medical intervention may be necessary and may bring many benefits far outweighing the costs. There are some excellent and trustworthy medics and paramedics out there, who will inform and support us as parents, as well as helping our children. When you find such a person, keep tabs on them! Even if they move to a different area or hospital, try to maintain contact, because they may be able to help down the road when things are getting rocky. I have been moved recently to contact one such medic, just to say thank you. I remember being impressed with his thoughtfulness and respectful attitude, but it was only after years of rather less helpful treatment that I fully appreciated his contribution. I think in all walks of life, we are more likely to receive criticism than thanks, even if doctors do occasionally receive undue adulation.

But then there *are* medical practitioners who worry us. Perhaps they are too ready to encourage us to get rid of our children, *in utero* or after birth. Perhaps they are too ready to use surgery or drugs. Perhaps they are too quick to assume that we cannot appreciate our offspring as they are. Whatever the reason for own unease might be, our children are absolutely dependent on our own strength of character to struggle to reach wise decisions, for even if we are consulting them, it takes a great deal of assertiveness to establish the facts, put them in a way our child can understand and come to an agreement. We and our children, after all, are going to be the ones to live out the consequences, so all our efforts are meaningful. Of course, we may still make mistakes, make decisions we live to regret, but if we have done our best then that is a great consolation. It is also a fundamental human right to learn from our mistakes. True enough we would not wish our children to suffer from our mistakes, but I think young people are capable of being very philosophical. They know when, in essence, you are an ally and they accept that in the face of enormous decisions, mistakes might be made. As long as mistakes are made in the midst of love and genuine respect, they can be swallowed.

This depends on our self-esteem as well. Some of us feel intimidated just going to see our GPs, let alone a consultant. We owe it to our children to overcome this, to demand that things be explained to us in ways that we can understand so that in our turn we can explain them to our children. And whenever possible we should stay with our children for hospital appointments and hospital stays. That way we have the best chance of protecting them from abusive medical systems, institutions and individuals.

Chapter Seven

Our Children in School

I, along with most of the disability movement, consider segregated schools, or so-called special schools, to be rather dangerous places.[1] They mostly represent, in a very concrete way, society's rejection of disabled people, and many disabled children are well aware of that. So are habitual perpetrators of abuse. Special schools are frequently miles from the parents' home and day journeys are long and tiring; residential placement means dislocation of the child and the whole family's life patterns. In the case of separate schools for deaf children, however, they represent the deaf community's rejection of mainstream schooling. It *is* difficult to see how a child whose natural language is sign language can function in an institution using spoken language which the child cannot acquire or cannot hear.

Equally, however, I reject the idea of throwing one disabled child into a mainstream school, with little provision to meet their needs, and calling that integration. There are ways in which this is as damaging to the child as segregation, and at least in a segregated setting they are with other young people who regard them as normal, rather than abnormal. In segregated settings there is some chance of developing 'disability pride' with one's peers.

But this is not the place for a debate about education. Plenty has already been written about the destructive effects of segregation, and the vision of inclusive education – a system planned and designed to include absolutely everyone on their own terms.[2] This chapter will concentrate on what happens to our children in both segregated and mainstream schools, and what needs to be done to improve how they are protected.

I am sure that the reason I was never teased or bullied in my first schools (a primary and secondary school run by a particularly good order of nuns), is that the nuns respected both my parents and myself. With the exception of one nun in the primary school who seemed to live in terror of my having accidents, I was not aware of any negative attitudes towards me, or of being singled out in any way. Indeed it seems as if the nuns tried very hard not to limit me. One of my favourite stories is of them watching with bated breath as I followed the line of my friends doing a balancing trick around the narrow edge of the school pond. I had no idea we were even being watched and it was not until years later that my parents told me how the group of nuns looking on breathed a united sigh of relief as I safely departed with the gang.

In my next school, however, things were utterly different. The headmistress announced to the whole school before I arrived, 'There's a cripple coming, and you are not to stare, not to laugh and not to point.' Her attitude, needless to say, poisoned the atmosphere for me in relation to the other children and, as seriously, to

some of the staff. Even in the sixth form there was the
weekly spectacle of my chemistry teacher asking
tenderly, 'Are you all right now dear?' so that I found
myself desperately searching my memory for time off for
sickness, and felt a great curtain of irritation fall
between me and my classmates. There was the gym
teacher who wouldn't let me play for the school tennis
team, even though I qualified week after week. There
was the trudge from my physics class where the teacher
berated me for not doing more for myself, to the maths
class where I was told I should let the other girls help
me more.

This absolutely *had* to have a knock-on effect on the
majority of other pupils. Many simply seemed to feel that
I had descended from a distant planet and didn't know
how to handle me. Some were friendly, but excluded me
from everyday teenage talk. One gave me hell.

The point I am making then, is that how the Head, in
particular, behaves towards disabled and other pupils, is
far and away the most important factor determining the
treatment that will be meted out by staff and non-
disabled pupils. It matters how they treat disabled pupils
because of the precedent it sets for everyone else. It
matters how they treat other pupils because if they are
dictatorial and disrespectful of students in general, the
latter will be looking for someone else to take it out on,
and disabled pupils are sometimes the easiest targets.

This, then applies to both mainstream and segregated
schools. A Head who is respectful of staff is likely to be
respectful of students too, and will at least be open to
advice about how to behave towards disabled students.

There are some things that all schools could usefully
teach their children, and which disabled young people in
particular tend to need help with. For instance, there is
the issue of children's rights. Most disabled young people
have picked up the idea that they have no rights; they

must just accept everything with a smile. They lack clarity about some things that most other young people learn quite early. For instance, because some physiotherapy and/or medical treatments are painful, they may not be clear that people do not normally have a right to hurt them. The emphasis on accepting what comes your way, to prove how well-adjusted you are, creates an atmosphere in which young disabled people feel they have *no right* to complain about mistreatment, regardless of whether or not they could overcome their fear of reprisals. And because our children are too often treated with profound disrespect (for instance when they are talked about, over their heads, or moved about without consultation), they need explicit teaching about the need to treat and be treated with respect.

If schools were to originate charters such as the one developed at Chailey Heritage in East Sussex, or teach about children's rights, it would be an enormous boost for young disabled people, who could subsequently recognise whether or not they were being treated as they should be. Also, to discuss these issues in a mainstream school would be incredibly helpful to non-disabled children both in terms of understanding their own rights, and in terms of opening their eyes to the lives of their disabled counterparts.

Segregated Schools

In 'Places of Safety?' Ruth Marchant and I raised the painful question of how safe segregated schools are likely to be.[3] Although this may be extremely worrying for some readers, it is not my intention to scaremonger. Unfortunately the truth is that if you ask a group of experienced child protection workers to describe the perfect job for a persistent perpetrator of abuse, the institution they describe, and the children within it, fit in with many aspects of our segregated schools. Thus they describe a place where the children are particularly vulnerable, easily silenced, and isolated both from their families and from the rest of society.

There are other features of the 'perfect' target institution, relating very much to leadership style and the usual ethos of the place, which will vary widely, so this should not be taken to mean that I think that *every* institution for disabled children is a hotbed of abuse! The key issue is that regardless of the calibre of the leadership and the staff, regardless of the quality of the policies and procedures laid down, much more effort needs to be made to protect disabled children in residential schools than might be necessary for other children. Even non-disabled children in residential schools, who are definitely facing a higher risk than most children living at home, can not be as vulnerable to abuse as disabled children, mainly because perpetrators need to ensure secrecy and silence.

Also, since we are not talking about sexual abuse alone, we need to remember that institutions for disabled children are much more likely to develop practices that are unacceptable, that is, institutional abuse. There are three reasons for this. The first is that staff, too, are relatively isolated and in these circumstances, practices and attitudes can warp because, without people having anything with which to compare, they can be unaware that they have diverted from any norms. The second is that it is extremely rare to find individuals, let alone staff groups anywhere, who apply the same standards to disabled children as they do to non-disabled children. It is also easy to fail to 'translate' actions such as punishments, taken with disabled youngsters into equivalent actions with non-disabled children (see page 144). The third reason is that anyone who works with disabled children tends to carry some of the stigma attached to the children. Thus staff are often underpaid; the care staff in particular are likely to be unskilled and receive little or no training. It isn't unheard of that teaching staff who can't cope in mainstream schools are reallocated to schools or units for disabled children.

In 'Out of Sight, Out of Mind', Sally French recounts the stories of several girls in a residential school for partially sighted and blind children.[4] I quote a few passages:

> None of us were ever comforted or even given a kind word. As we got older we could adapt to it but the little ones needed comfort and no one ever gave it to them. I didn't like them being ill-treated, I didn't like them being hit, they were away from home and they were unhappy. I saw it happen so much I used to feel sorry for the little kids when I got older.

> They would often say we were appalling girls, always scruffy and untidy. We were told off for the most simple things, a sock down was really frowned upon. I never ever remember them praising us for anything.

Both of these illustrate institutional emotional abuse. That is, it was not just one cold member of staff, but had become institutional practice. Furthermore, this was going on at the same time that I was at school, not in some bygone era when we might have expected such harsh treatment of children away from home. It is interesting that these women recall that parents were treated equally coldly – no welcoming cups of tea for instance, and then criticised in the hearing of the children after they had left. And yet parents apparently were also intimidated into inaction. As French states, this abuse had inevitable repercussions and some of it is extremely relevant for us.

> The abuse that the girls received led many to abscond from the school (Monkhouse, 1980). We could all

remember how in January 1960 two girls, aged 11 and
12, ran away in the night and were missing for two full
days. They were found 100 miles from the school after
receiving a lift from a lorry driver who sexually
assaulted them many times. (*Daily Express*, 30
January 1960; *Peterborough Citizen and Advertiser*, 3
February 1960) . . . In answer to these accusations [of
a cover up] she [the principal] said 'I have given twenty
years of my life to these girls – how can it be said that
I don't care?'(*Wokingham Times*, 5 February 1960).

And French illustrates well how social attitudes colluded
in silencing not only these particular girls, but any
concern about the school:

No enquiry of the school took place. In fact their
behaviour was interpreted as a futile attempt to 'prove'
to themselves that their partial sight was not a
handicap (*Daily Mail*, 29 January 1960).

Some of these children told their parents about the abuse
and were disbelieved. Others didn't tell in order to
protect parents from the worry, given that they were so
far away. This means that the children perceived their
parents as powerless, perhaps a result of the staff
criticising parents behind their backs and keeping them
at a distance. We begin to see just how powerful an
institution can be and are reminded that abuse is all
about the misuse of power.

This theme, of institutional abuse occurring and being
covered up with ease in residential schools for disabled
people, is one that recurs down the years. Again that is
not to suggest that there is such abuse in every residential
'special' school, but it is much more prevalent than the
general public realise. What we have to remember is that
it is exactly their residential nature, and the fact that they
are often far from children's homes, that allows abusive
practice to develop and flourish. It is much less likely in

a day school, with people coming and going creating more opportunity for outside scrutiny.

We also need to remember, however, that abuse by individuals can happen in an institution and that it may go undetected if a number of factors are mitigating against the child:

- If the child can't tell because of communication difficulties of whatever kind.
- If the child won't tell for fear of the repercussions.
- If the perpetrator is in a powerful position within the institution.
- If the ethos of the place is staff vs children.
- If the perpetrator has the classic qualities of outward charm, and is popular with the staff.
- If the staff as a whole are not trained to look out for signs and indicators.
- If the institution lacks any or adequate Child Protection policies and procedures.
- If the institution lacks Intimate Care policies and procedures.
- If the institution is run by a powerful organisation such as a major charity, which has the wherewithal to keep concerns under wraps, and puts its image above all else.

It should be emphasised that all is definitely not lost if the child cannot communicate with anyone what has happened. It is not uncommon for disabled children to disclose on behalf of each other. And sometimes visiting professionals, like psychologists, who are not employed full-time at the school, might do the whistle-blowing. But if several of the other factors are in place then disclosure might not produce the desired results.

Segregated schools must also look at training issues. Most local authorities will admit that when they first began to train teachers about Child Protection, they missed out the staff in 'special schools' because they thought disabled children weren't at risk. As this omission was increasingly challenged, staff at 'special' schools began to get places on training courses, but came away feeling none the wiser, for the cources were not designed with disabled children in mind and were of minimal relevance. It is really only since the publication of the 'Abuse and Children who are Disabled' training pack that staff anywhere have received appropriate, in-depth training. Even so, education departments are relatively slow on the uptake and my colleagues and I tend to find just one or two teachers on any of our courses.

Punishments

Parents and carers may be more aware than the general public of how easy it is to inflict extremely cruel punishments on disabled children, and get away with it. Many, many people have confirmed that punishments such as removal of a communication board, or removal of a battery from an electric wheelchair are common-place. These are the equivalent of gagging a non-disabled child, or tying a non-disabled child's legs together, neither of which are legal. Yet the authorities have not bothered to explore this area, perhaps because they still believe in the stereotype of all parents and carers as patient 'saints'. Equally I doubt that the practice of tying deaf children's hands behind their backs to stop them from signing has completely died out in schools persisting with the oral tradition.

Not that long ago I was training some workers in a voluntary organisation supporting parents of disabled children. They told me of a mother of a boy with learning difficulties who discovered in the worst possible way that staff at his school routinely punished children by denying them their lunch. How did she find out? Her child kept coming home and eating stones out in the garden. This punishment is illegal, and the advocacy workers backed up this mother's insistence that it be stopped.

I do not want to present a gruesome chronicle of all the punishments I have encountered being inflicted on disabled children. The point is that we need to know what the school does and doesn't allow, before giving over the care of our children. We also need to listen to our children and let them know they can tell us about anything that upsets them.

This is also true of restraint methods, both in terms of the methods used to control children whose behaviour is a danger to themselves or others and the kinds of restraints designed to prevent injury. This was highlighted by the case in which a child with cerebral palsy was tied on to his bed face down by straps attached to all four limbs. Video evidence emerged and was plastered all over our television screens. Certainly restraining children who are behaving dangerously is not easy, but there are training courses available and it should not be left to the ingenuity – or brutality – of staff to devise their own methods.

One tradition in segregated schools that must be challenged forcefully, is that of having open days. Disabled young people, if they feel safe enough to be honest, experience these as little more than freak shows. There is absolutely nothing wrong with an open day, held when the children are not attending, where their achievements are on display and specialist equipment can be shown off, and such an open day would surely still be able to bring great credit to the school. Voyeurism is a very particular kind of abuse to which disabled children tend to be subjected both in professional arenas (doctors displaying children to their colleagues, whilst giving a lecture on the child's condition) and in public places. It is intolerable to expect disabled children to put up with this *ever*, let alone once a year, in a place which is supposed to be empowering them through education.

Mainstream schools

The problems disabled children might encounter in mainstream schools are of a different order. Because the institution is, as I have already said, relatively transparent to public gaze, and also because staff are generally better trained as teachers and in relation to Child Protection, and usually have higher morale, it is often other pupils who are abusive, rather than staff.

The main problem facing teachers is their lack of training on disability issues. All too often, in these days of assimilation masquerading as integration, disabled children are dumped in teachers' classrooms and the teachers have little or no idea about adapting their methods or classrooms. They assume that if a child is there they are supposed to mix in and manage like the others, unless they have a statement to say otherwise. But where the statement requires schools to provide support staff, the teacher often assumes that the support staff have all the expertise necessary and can just get on with the job. So, often, staff make the learning environment extremely difficult for disabled children, without actually intending to do so.

One of the girls I work with told me this:

My PE teacher is stupid. She won't listen to me when I tell her I can't play hockey. She expects me to just stand there for an hour in case a ball comes my way and I might be able to hit it. I've asked her to give me something else to do and she won't. Carol [her sister, not her real name] is allowed to do homework during PE but she won't let me. So I've just said 'Blow this' and I sit on my bum for the whole two periods. It's just stupid!

It is far from impossible to make PE inclusive, and there are videos to assist staff to do this, produced by the National Sports Council.

I recall one girl who was bright, sociable and deaf. She might have coped in a mainstream school had her teachers not signally failed to do the things they had been asked to do, in order to make the classroom environment accessible. This not only meant that this girl was doing much less well academically than she should, it also became a model of contempt for the other pupils. She was subjected to bullying and was finally too miserable to continue. Her eventual choice of a school for deaf children where sign language was used and where she could feel proud of herself as deaf, meant that she flourished socially and academically.

School support workers

The school support worker plays rather an odd role. In theory this position is excellent, providing the one-to-one support a child may need to function in a mainstream setting. In practice it is fraught with problems, and support workers can easily become a thorn in the flesh of the children to whom they should be allies. Some comments have been:

It's that Tessa [not her real name] again. I had an argument with my friend, and the next thing I know Tessa is telling me off in front of other people, and saying I have to make it up and it's not nice to argue! The others can fall out and that's that!

I don't believe that woman. She's supposed to be helping me and she's telling me off when I get things wrong!

Do you know what she did? She told someone else's Mum that I was being rude on the bus, saying things I never said at all. She's just a troublemaker.

All these comments reveal a major source of the difficulties. On the one hand these workers have a role that involves invading the child's world. There is usually a clear 'Them and Us' of children and teachers, not necessarily a negative distinction at all, but a well-defined one nevertheless. The teacher cannot be privy to the little pranks and confidences, the tides of friendship and battle, but a support worker is right in the thick of it. Without clear guidelines about the proper boundaries of their role (and I've never heard of such guidelines being issued), they can become not just an irritant to the disabled child, but a monumental barrier between them and their non-disabled classmates. As another girl pointed out to me:

> She [the support worker] is supposed be there for Clare, I don't have a need for a support worker in my statement. But that doesn't stop her coming over to me and trying to give me help. It's really embarrassing.

This behaviour makes it quite impossible for disabled young people to be taken seriously by their peers and really makes a mockery of the whole attempt at inclusion.

Bullying

As Phillipa Russell, Director of the Council for Disabled Children, pointed out to me:

> One or two of the major studies on bullying (particularly one in Sheffield) found that disabled children and children with special educational needs were more likely to be bullied than other children. But the Sheffield study hypothesised that bullying was not inevitable; that it can be prevented (or at least dealt with) and perhaps [these] children are actually less likely to be taught or acquire the streetwise skills that often protect other children.'

She also mentioned some innovative projects which have included disabled children, designed to tackle bullying, and encouragingly:

> The DFEE (Department for Education and Employment) launched a pack on bullying (suggesting positive remedies) a year or so ago and schools are now expected to have active policies on bullying. Many to their credit have gone beyond that and involve pupils themselves in prevention strategies and dealing with actual cases.

But what form does the bullying take and how much does it matter? Taking the last question first, we have all heard stories of young people who were bullied to the extent that they have taken their own lives. This tells us clearly that bullying is abuse which is given another name, perhaps because it goes on between peers. In the light of the amount of attention that is now being paid to peer abuse, however, particularly in relation to young people with learning difficulties, there is probably a case for suggesting that bullying be renamed as abuse to highlight the gravity of its effects, and to minimise the differences between this and other abuse. Surely, very often, the only difference is that the perpetrator, still much more powerful than the victim, is another child.

The school bully operates no differently from an adult perpetrator. They target vulnerable children, children who are physically weak, emotionally vulnerable or isolated for whatever reason, and easily silenced or disbelieved. They hurt their victims emotionally, physically, or both, and always terrify and threaten. The threats, just like an adult's, include terrible consequences for telling. As an increasing number of people have realised all this, more and more schools now take the problem of bullying very seriously. Unfortunately, the myth that no one would abuse a disabled child applies here too, so that adults often find it harder to believe a disabled child who says they are being bullied, than a non-disabled child. Also, disabled young people have sometimes been told they should be able to take this behaviour, presumably to demonstrate how well-adjusted they are. However, it is good to remember that if we help our children build up their self-esteem, this can provide a protective cloak against a bully who preys on others' insecurities.

I would guess, from listening to disabled children, that a good proportion of the bullying is name-calling. Children, we all know, can be either tedious or extremely creative in the names they make up. Either way, if you know that each time you make an appearance in the playground, one or more of your peers will be shouting out endless abuse, it is hard to hold your head up. Indeed, bullies are never satisfied until their victim is in tears.

But some of the bullying is indeed physical. Tales of children who wear glasses having them removed and smashed on the ground are not new. Children who use wheelchairs can find themselves being pushed at high speed to places they don't want to go. One girl I know, who can walk but is unsteady, was consistently knocked over by a bully in the playground and then was accused by teachers of being clumsy and not looking where she was going!

If staff model disrespectful, if not contemptuous behaviour towards disabled pupils, non-disabled pupils are highly likely to produce from amongst their number at least a few who will take this as carte blanche for bullying. It has an exact parallel with racism and of course children experiencing multiple oppression are the most likely to be targeted.

Transport

Another problem that is closely connected with protecting our children from abuse is the matter of how they are transported to school.

Now it is almost certain that any transport approved by a local authority will be physically safe. That is, the vehicles will be in a good state of repair and there will be wheelchair restraints and so on. What is less certain is how safe the personnel involved might be.

Abuse by drivers and escorts is, sadly, not uncommon. And the danger is at its gravest with private taxi firms. For some reason there is a loophole in the law, so that taxi drivers do not have to be police checked, even if they are taking children to and from school (or anywhere else). It has been known for a Schedule One offender (that is, someone previously jailed for sexual offences against children), to run a taxi firm and employ only other Schedule One offenders.

Although this is alarming, and ought to be tackled by the authorities, we should try not to panic if our children are indeed travelling without us. Most of us feel that the moment we wave goodbye is the moment we can relax a little and think our own thoughts, or look after our own needs a little more. And so it should remain, for once the child is on the transport there is nothing we can do. On the other hand there are lots of things we can do to reduce the risk, and many are covered in previous chapters, such as maximising the child's communication skills and self-esteem, and being alert for distress before or after journeys. It also emphasises the need for good awareness on the part of the school and good communication between them and ourselves. But just being aware that there could be a problem is the first and most important thing.

Find out all you can

As with medical intervention, the key to successfully protecting our children lies in gathering as much information as possible.

Questions to ask segregated schools

In segregated schools, if the danger comes from being away from the public gaze, then as parents and carers, we have to make sure that we place the school under the closest scrutiny we can. We can do this both by visiting our children and observing, and by asking questions.

1. May I see your Child Protection policy and procedures? Are these sent out to all parents? Whether or not we are shown a copy, we need to know: What does it have to say about notifying parents when there is an allegation or suspicion of abuse? Would we be notified immediately? What should happen if they were concerned about the child's transport from home? What would they do in the event of a suspicion that a member of staff might be abusing children in their care? At what point would we be told if our own child had sustained an injury or was ill, or was at the centre of concerns? At what point would we be told if someone else's child was at the centre of concerns? Who is the named teacher for Child Protection issues? (Regulations state that each school must have one teacher who is named as the co-ordinator in the school in relation to child protection. Staff with concerns are supposed to discuss these first with the named teacher.)
2. Do you have any Intimate Care policy and procedures? Do all staff have copies? Do all parents get copies? Are they explained as far as possible to the children?
3. If my child wants to get in touch with me urgently and privately, is there a way they can do that?

4. Do the staff receive training in detecting signs and indicators of abuse? If so, is it specifically geared to disabled children?
5. Is there any complaints procedure for the children?
6. Do you hold open days? If so are the children absent or present?
7. What guidelines exist for staff about punishment and restraints? Can I have a copy?
8. Do you have a charter of children's rights and/or teach the children about their rights?

Schools that have no answers, or try to deflect the questions, or challenge your right to ask the questions or know the answers are suspect. I have carefully said 'schools' in the last sentence because one defensive individual is not a whole school. The individual may be suspect, but we should not worry until we have met the same barrier from senior staff including the Head.

Questions to ask in mainstream schools

1. Have your staff in general, and the named teacher for child protection in particular, had any training relating specifically to protecting disabled children from abuse?
2. Do you have a policy on bullying? If so, does it address issues for disabled children?
3. Is there a complaints procedure for disabled children and their parents, in respect of mistreatment by teachers or school support workers?
4. Is there written policy and procedures with respect to intimate care, for school support workers?
5. Have staff had any disability equality training?
6. Do you have a charter of children's rights and/or teach the children about their rights?

It can be quite difficult to ask these questions and sometimes we can encounter quite defensive reactions. It may be helpful to present the questions as a printed sheet as this can seem less confrontational. Any answers we receive will be invaluable in helping us promote our child's interests.

Section Three
Recognising and Dealing with Abuse

Part Three
Reasoning and Decision-making
in law

Chapter Eight

Signs and Indicators of Abuse in Disabled Children

Recognising early signs and indicators of abuse can mean the difference between early action to put a stop to further abuse and trauma for the child, and a discovery that comes too late to prevent even more serious damage. Regrettably, of course, recognising these signals doesn't prevent abuse taking place in the first instance, but if others notice that we are alert to the indicators of abuse, it adds a further protective layer around our children.

There is a yawning abyss between the referral rate for suspected abuse of disabled children and the likely numbers abused. There are many reasons for this, but one is that people often miss the signs and indicators that would be picked up if the child were non-disabled, or spot them but attribute them to almost anything *but* abuse.

Fundamentally the signs and indicators of abuse are not different for our disabled children. Gerrilyn Smith details them thoroughly in *The Protector's Handbook* and in *ABCD*, and her charts of indicators are included in Appendix II.[1] Although her book deals exclusively with sexual abuse, many of the signs and indicators she refers to occur in response to other kinds of abuse too. For example, person or situation specific fears, nightmares and bed-wetting could be indicators of any kind of abuse. We can add things like unexplained or improbably explained injuries, flinching, neglected appearance, chronic hunger and failure to thrive. Also, signs and indicators of one suspected kind of abuse can sometimes uncover other maltreatment. So a child who is physically brutalised in order to allow the pursuit of sexual acts may well have unexplained bruising. Low self-esteem is the result of any kind of abuse. Unfortunately, as we have previously explored, disability oppression also tends to produce low self-esteem, so these are muddy waters.

Just to summarise, Gerrilyn Smith lists common signs and indicators of abuse, but she also groups them according to the likelihood that they result from abuse, dividing them into Blue (lots of other possible explanations), Green (still quite a number of possible explanations but a higher level of concern) and Red (few possible explanations other than abuse). Smith further divides these to indicate not only how signs and indicators vary cross three major age groups (under 5, 5–12 and 12 upwards), but also how their *significance* may alter across each of these age groups. Thus, sexually transmitted diseases in children under 12 are much more alarming than in the over 12 age group, because the latter may have had consenting, albeit illegal, sex.

Different life experiences

Useful as the above is, the most obvious problem for us is that children who are disabled sometimes have very different life experiences so that the significance of any sign (that is, whether it should be regarded as a blue, green or red indicator) may be very different. Thus, at the extreme, a non-disabled teenager who becomes pregnant may well have had consenting sex. Disabled teenagers do tend to be over-protected, and are often lucky just to get out alone. If they do, they rarely manage to take part in the teenage scene, either because of the attitude of their non-disabled counterparts, or because of the inaccessibility of 'teen-scene' venues. Equally, boyfriends and girlfriends are a much more fraught issue for disabled teenagers and their parents alike. So a teenager who is disabled and becomes pregnant *may* have had consenting sex, but it is much less probable, and so straightforward abuse is a more likely explanation.

On the other hand, it is also true that the different life experiences of our children do cause 'symptoms' which are actually *not* the result of abuse. For example, badly fitting equiment or ill designed aids can cause bruising and abrasions. I was once given a caliper of which the bucket top (the part that fitted round the thigh) was made of a new plastic. No one (including myself) had noticed that the upper edge had been cut at an angle, resulting in a finish which could have passed as a kitchen knife. It shredded me the first, and last, time I wore it. It may have been abusive practice that allowed it to be given to me like that, but it would only have become abuse if people had failed to correct the problem once it had been identified.

Equally, there are times when new medications or doses have undesired effects, and when new exercise regimes unsettle and temporarily upset our children. So we must be level-headed, as must others, when we spot possible signs and indicators. As parents and carers we should just look out for any obvious non-abuse explanations before we start to worry. The problem is not, historically, that people have failed to look for such explanations; instead they have actually manufactured them rather than face the possibility that abuse may have occurred.

Neglect

Neglect deserves our particular attention as it appears to be the most common form of abuse of disabled children, judging by Crosse Kaye and Ratnofsky's findings and by what I and my colleagues have picked up over the years.[2] Some neglect is no different from that of non-disabled children; some arises out of an ignorance of the needs of the particular child; some is quite wilful neglect of the impairment based and/or medical needs of the child. In other words, some parents and carers are fully aware of what the child needs, over and above what any child might need, but are simply not prepared to fulfil that responsibility.

Unfortunately, especially in the case of children with complex or profound impairments, the signs and indicators may well be overlooked because so few of the behaviours or so little of the child's appearance starts out like that of a non-disabled child.

The most commonly neglected need is for stimulation, especially of the senses that are intact. Too many parents and carers don't see the point of stimulating their children, because they secretly harbour the attitude that the child is useless. In fact, by neglecting them they can render them comparatively 'useless', where they may not otherwise have been so.

Children who are desperately under-stimulated are especially likely to rock or self-injure (for example by head-banging), in order to feel something. They are especially likely to have emotionally blank expressions and may be frightened by interaction or touch. Skills they should have been able to acquire will be absent. And this is where it takes real co-operation between those who know a lot about the child and the impairment, and those who know a lot about child protection, to unravel the cause of the child's behaviour.

Fewer behaviours, fewer signs and indicators

In Gerrilyn Smith's list for children over 12 there are a number of behaviours that would be difficult for some disabled children and impossible for others, regardless of what they might *wish* they could do. Thus arson is quite a common way that non-disabled teenagers tell us how angry and disturbed they are. Obviously, some disabled youngsters would find this difficult just because they are rarely unsupervised, or are never out on their own. Others would simply find it a physical impossibility. Again, some disabled children may wish they could run away, or steal or scavenge, but for the vast majority these are not viable options. Perhaps the child who cannot commit arson is doing lots of pictures of things going up in flames. Perhaps they are telling violent stories. Perhaps they are just permanently screaming, difficult and tense.

The limited nature of a child's behavioural repertoire can lead to confusion. One behaviour, like crying, may mean many things. Certainly I have met at least one truly loving and concerned mother who missed her son's attempts to show her something was wrong. This boy cried loudly every time he had to return to school at the end of the weekend with the family. He understood much of what was said to him but only had Yes/No signals with which to respond. His mother simply assumed that he had enjoyed himself so much at home that he was reluctant to leave. Without being asked specifically 'Is there anything bad happening at school that is making you upset?', he had no way of communicating the abuse.

She only found out as it became apparent that several other pupils had also been abused.

If a child's range of possible behaviours is very limited, so will be their range of ways in which they can express their feelings. This means we have to be much more alert.

What to look out for

Signs of distress occurring at the change from one setting or activity to another (home to school; school to school bus; school to physiotherapy) are one way in which many disabled children signal that something is wrong, and should therefore be noted. If it happens once it may not be a cause for concern. If it happens often it should be investigated further.

Equally we should note signs of distress arising in relation to contact with any particular person, whether carer or professional. Sometimes the child is fearful in advance, or cries and becomes difficult. Sometimes the child is desperately unsettled after contact with the person and takes hours or even days to settle back to their normal selves. Finally we should notice if the signs of distress occur at particular times – bath-time or bedtime, for example.

Another way to look at the subtleties is to think in terms of the meaning of signs and indicators, given the child's existing behavioural repertoire. In other words, the significance of any new or different behaviour can only be assessed within the context of the ways that the child *can* behave. A small change can signal a large problem if the child cannot do many unassisted things in the first place. Take withdrawal. This is a common reaction to any kind of abuse. In a non-disabled child it may take the form of hanging around in corners of the playground at breaks, instead of their previous behaviour of joining in vigorous games with their friends. A child with extremely limited mobility may always be dependent on others as to whether or not they are with their friends and therefore may not be able to withdraw physically from friendship groups. Equally, if their most active behaviour involves only head and eye movements, then withdrawal is going to be signalled very differently and much more subtly. It may be that the child makes eye contact only if it is demanded and not otherwise. It may be that all smiles have gone. For example, a colleague of mine reported being concerned when one girl with cerebral palsy came in for her regular hearing check. Usually this girl had her head up and was bright and alert. On this occasion her head never left her chest. Alarmed, my colleague asked the father what had happened and he lifted the girl's clothing to reveal bite marks all over her back, replying that staff at school had not prevented another child from biting her.

We must therefore be alert to all changes in our children's behaviour and appearance and not dismiss it just because in non-disabled terms it may be such a small change. If you witness one of these changes you need to note everything possible about it: when it started, when it eases or gets worse; whether or not there is a more obvious likely cause (like a family upset or change of school). Then it is wise to acknowledge to the child that you have noticed this change. If you are concerned about what may be causing it because you are not aware of any problems in the child's life, sharing your concern with the child will not go amiss, and may allow the child to indicate in more detail what is wrong, or simply to let go of some of the distress.

I heard recently about a mother who could not put her finger on what was the matter with her multiply impaired child. She just knew something was wrong. She took her daughter to hospital and badgered the doctors until they brought in a paediatrician experienced in relation to abuse. When this paediatrician said to the mother that in her opinion there were signs of abuse, the mother said, 'Oh God. I came home early the other day from bingo and found my husband crouched over my daughter, who was completely naked, on the living room floor. He said he was just changing her because she was wet.'

Since signs and indicators with our children may be so much more subtle, Marchant and Page say:

> When assessing possible signs of abuse with disabled children it is important to combine an adult's personal knowledge of the changes in the child's usual behaviour or emotional state with the specialist knowledge of relevant professionals who can assess the significance of those signs given the child's age, developmental stage and particular disability.[3]

In other words we need to hear from people who are very familiar with the child's day-to-day ways, but also from people like speech and language therapists and physiotherapists as well as child protection social workers, to get the clearest possible perspective.

How signs and indicators in disabled children get explained away

Naturally, perpetrators of abuse, particularly those for whom it is a way of life, become adept at providing plausible explanations for the signs of abuse. Child protection workers tend to have been made well aware of these excuses for non-disabled children. When it comes to disabled children, however, they can fall victim to a number of explanations which hold no water, simply because of a lack of understanding of what disability is all about.

Thus there is the tendency amongst the public and professionals alike to attribute signs and indicators of abuse to the impairment itself. I have heard speech and language therapists, for example, say things like 'Well, children with Down's syndrome *do* masturbate, don't they?' as if it were somehow part of the syndrome and only to be expected. Another popular one is: 'Blind children do masturbate a lot; they need the stimulation'! Needless to say these are complete nonsense. If such assumptions are based in any reality it will be the reality that disabled children are so much more likely to have been abused and are showing it through behaviours such as excessive masturbation, rather than these 'symptoms' being inherent in their condition.

Before disability and child protection were ever included on the official agenda, I remember running a course for play workers and respite carers. I invited them to tell me about behaviours they found difficult to understand or manage. Two respite workers then told me about a seven-year-old boy who had learning difficulties who would literally tear incontinence pads or nappies off other children so that he could wear them, rub himself against them and get an erection. When, I asked what they thought it was about, they said, 'Well, he has learning difficulties, he just doesn't understand that you don't do that.' And when I suggested that it indicated to me the possibility that he had been abused (for this is sexualised behaviour), they were angry and disgusted with me (an occupational hazard!).

Another way that signs and indicators are conveniently explained away is by making use of the common confusion between disability and illness. That is, when someone raises a concern about a particular disabled child, they are met with a statement like 'Oh, she's just not very well at the moment' or, more powerfully, 'It's just the medication.' These statements are often accepted at face value, especially when, as is too often the case, they come from a GP.

One social worker realised with dismay how willingly she had accepted a GP's explanation of a disabled child's anus gaping whenever his incontinence pad was changed. The GP had assured her it was due to the child having rectal Valium. It was only when the foster mother reported six months after the placement had begun (following the imprisonment of his parents and grandfather for abusing his brothers and sisters) that he still had rectal Valium but the gaping had stopped, that she realised she had accepted the GP's word because it was too painful to contemplate that what she had seen in the photographs of his siblings could have happened to him too.

This means we have to be wary and sometimes follow our gut reactions and persist in our attempts to get at the truth, if we suspect we have been given a too glib, or false explanation. It also means we need to be familiar with how medication does and does not affect our children, so that we can highlight changes for others.

Rather akin to explaining signs and indicators away by implying they are part and parcel of the impairment, is the other great non-statement (which in my own experience is the most readily accepted), which is 'S/he has always been like that. Don't worry about it.' I have heard this over and over again, particularly in relation to behaviours like boys grabbing female staff's breasts or putting their hands up these women's skirts. Now it is true that this is not something that anyone could get away with telling you if *you* have always been the parent or carer of this child, but if you have fostered or adopted the child, or are taking them for respite, you might well hear it. Again, it bears no scrutiny whatsoever, but what happens is that people who have known the child the shortest length of time feel they have no right to question the knowledge or experience of one who has known them longer.

For staff in institutions, there is also the issue of not questioning the judgement of more senior or long-serving staff. I am aware that this has left many children in situations where they are abused right up to adulthood, by which time any kind of intervention is exceptionally difficult.

Another popular way of persuading people to forget about signs and indicators is to say, 'Oh it's just their way of getting some attention.' Now whilst this excuse may also be heard by child protection workers in the case of non-disabled children, they are more likely to accept it when the child is disabled. They are more ready to believe (a) that a disabled child receives too little attention and (b) that they will indulge in attention-seeking behaviours. Frankly, if someone tells *me* that a child is attention seeking then I immediately want to know why. Why does this child need attention? Do they get too little? If so, how can that be remedied? Or is this child trying to tell us something? If so, what?

Finally we must be alert to people explaining that physical damage to the child's body was self-inflicted. Where children with leaning difficulties are concerned, people seem particularly prone to swallowing this rather extraordinary excuse. In the first place self-injuring is a *strong* sign of abuse! In the second place, this explanation has been offered in circumstances where the mechanics of it test the imagination. One young boy at an institution had friction burns on his back. Staff duly explained that he had done it to himself, but no one could really work out how. Then a night worker was spotted dragging the boy naked across the floor to his bed at bedtime. So frankly, if ever we are given this sort of explanation we should refer to Social Services immediately. On either count, something is wrong. There are a couple of extremely rare syndromes which involve self-injury, so there is some faint possibility that this might be the explanation. These children are distinctly relieved, rather than agitated, when they are put in restraints that prevent them from self-injuring. They are, however, so rare that in all my years of contact with disabled people I have never met anyone with these syndromes.

Finding out what is wrong

Given that a child may have little or no verbal communication, and sometimes very few possible behaviours, how can we find out what is bothering them? One key thing to do, which has already been noted, is to record usual behaviours, conditions and reactions in some detail so that we are aware when there is a change. If we are concerned we can ask others to tell us if they have noticed any change, and if so what, and/or in which circumstances. So at first, a teacher, for instance, might say, 'No, your little girl is just the same', but if asked whether she is the same at lunchtime, or before the transport is due, for instance, might then remember that they too have noticed her becoming fretful and tense.

If our child can understand a lot more than they can communicate back, a good rule of thumb is to acknowledge to the child that you have noticed that in such and such a situation, or with this particular person, they are no longer happy. This alone might provoke an outpouring of emotion that will tell you a great deal. If not, you could persist by saying that you are not happy to see that they have got a problem, and that whatever it is, you will try your very best to find out what it is and put a stop to it. This could provoke reactions of extreme fear if a child is being sexually abused and threatened by the perpetrator with terrible consequences if anyone should find out. But in this case you need to reassure the child over and over that nothing terrible will happen if you discover what has been going on and that any threats are probably lies. But we do need to uncover the threat, if possible, and expose it whilst acknowledging how frightening it was. Our children *are* very vulnerable and easily threatened and even more easily silenced. Any abused child needs a lot of reassurance that uncovering the truth will not mean that they, or others, are blamed and will also not mean that they will come to any harm.

In general, when disabled children are able to indicate that they have a problem, we need to learn to acknowledge their difficulty as a first step. Our own pain often gets in the way and we are too quick to reassure, leaving the child stranded with their struggle. For example, a very concerned and genuine young woman once asked me what she should do about her friend who was a wheelchair user. The friend had said she hated going out in public because she got stared at. I asked this young woman what she had done so far and she replied, 'I told her it was because she was so pretty.' Obviously the motivation was to comfort her friend, but ultimately it was a lie and would have been of no real comfort because when you are on the receiving end of staring you can't be fooled as to the cause! Had she said, 'Yes, people do stare, don't they. What would you like to do about it?', she and her friend could have devised strategies for dealing with the situation that would have been empowering for her friend and strengthening of their relationship.

If we habitually acknowledge rather than deny difficulties that our children face, even if we have to voice them first, they are much more likely to trust us to react appropriately if bad things are happening to them and give us every possible clue they can.

Don't panic

It is vital, though, that you remember that it is rare that *anyone* will assume abuse has taken place on the basis of one sign or indicator alone. Social Services have been given a really bad image as people who jump in and take children away on the slightest suspicion of abuse. At present, this is highly unlikely for non-disabled children and virtually inconceivable for our disabled children. No child is removed from the family now unless they are clearly in grave danger if they remain. This is extremely rare and requires the clearest of evidence. And whatever we do, we shouldn't stop showing affection to any of our children in case someone accuses us of abuse! Children need hugs and cuddles and kisses and doing this in a normal fashion can only do good. This is especially true of disabled children since they often miss out on the other aspects of social approval that help children to feel loved. This may relate directly to the child's impairment. If, for instance, our child is blind or partially sighted, they may not be aware of expressions on people's faces that show approval or appreciation. They may, if they have a hearing loss, be unaware of the delighted comments that are often passed to parents, and sometimes directed to the child themselves. On the other hand, disabled children are also the subject of disapproving stares. Comments range from the one most common in my childhood, 'Never mind about your leg, dear, at least you've got a pretty face' (a real double-edged sword that left me in terror of any damage to my face), to 'Shocking, to bring a child like that out on the streets' or, at worst, 'It would have been better if he'd died at birth, wouldn't it?'. All this makes tangible affection even more important.

Yes, it can be harder to teach a child with learning difficulties who they can hug and kiss and who they can't, but it is not impossible. On its own, and especially at younger ages or younger developmental levels, being rather indiscriminate about who you hug or kiss is not something that should arouse serious concern. It *only* arouses concern when the hugs and kisses are accompanied by groping hands or demands for sexual activity, or the child actively seeks out strangers who will fondle them.

Social workers and others are trained to look for non-abusive explanations of signs and indicators, and must fail to come up with any satisfactory explanations before concluding that an investigation of possible abuse might be necessary. For example, we all know that a child whose parents are in the process of splitting up may show disturbed behaviour, like withdrawal or food refusal, bed-wetting or aggression. A child whose pet has just died may become depressed and be unable to concentrate in class. Workers must look at all the possibilities because children show their distress about anything upsetting in their behaviour.

A perfect, if minor, example came up recently in some consultancy work I was doing. A foster carer told me that a 14-year-old boy's mother had always had him neatly turned out, but the mother had now left and he was in the care of his father. She was sure the father was neglecting him because he now arrived at weekends with holes in his trouser knees. It emerged, however, that since the mother had left, the lad had grown dramatically and with his new height and weight was no longer able to walk. He had therefore begun to get around on his knees . . . Fair enough, the father could have been advised about some sort of knee pads to protect the trousers, but here was a legitimate explanation for something that might otherwise have looked like one indicator of neglect.

So, if our child falls over and comes up in a lovely bruise, we shouldn't panic. We may just tell teachers, or other people who care for our child, what happened and discuss whether it was an accident that could be prevented another time, or just one of those things that may happen again. It is useful to have these discussions because sometimes we can't think of ways of preventing a recurrence because we're too close to it, or have little experience in relation to a child with this impairment. Others may be able to come up with really good ideas. Of course, the reverse might also be true. An accident may happen at school and we may be the ones who can suggest a way of preventing it happening again. A child has to sustain many bruises, especially in places that are unlikely to be hurt in accidents, before anyone will start to raise concerns (unless they are hand or fingertip shaped bruises) because, as one friend of mine would put it, it is a child's job to get bruises. It is part and parcel of learning about their bodies and the relationship of their bodies to the world.

It is clear that over-protection – denying our children normal experiences – has nothing to do with real protection. They need our affection, our attention and our respect. If we develop good parenting skills, then we will be able to tell when all is not well.

Chapter Nine

What to do if you Suspect Abuse

Some of you may have turned to this page before reading much of the rest of the book, having picked it up because you were already worried. If so, I strongly advise that you take the time to read through what has gone before because it will give you ideas about how and why things may have occurred and questions that should be asked. Also it will clarify the need to give those to whom you make a referral relevant information (such as the fact that the child requires intimate care). Finally you will be aware of some of the questions they should be pursuing.

Others will have become concerned after reading the information contained in previous chapters, and want to know what to do next. In this case, if some of the advice is difficult to follow now, for instance if detailed records weren't kept earlier, the best approximation you can manage will be helpful, and is certainly better than leaving the subject altogether. Others again will be reading this just to be informed should the need arise. Let's hope it doesn't.

First steps

If we are concerned for the first time, it is critical that we write down (and/or draw) all signs and indicators, stating how they came to our attention, and giving the dates and times. Although we are not necessarily concerned the first time, say, a bruise appears, we should make a written note in case it is the first of a worrying succession of indicators. Remember, investigators will rarely be bothered by a one-off unless it is something extremely serious (injuries requiring hospitalisation, or sexually transmitted diseases, for instance). If you are able to produce written accounts that are dated and timed, social workers in particular are not only likely to take you more seriously, they will also be much better equipped to move forward.

Observations preferred

Try very hard to record observations, rather than interpretations. For example, we may need to document that 'Jane always arrives home trembling and white.' That note would be useful to social workers. What we should not do is say that Jane is frightened of her transport driver. Many signs and indicators can have a multitude of different meanings and it is the investigating social worker's job to get to the bottom of it all.

Having said this, we can record our interpretations, *if* we say that this is what they are. For example, we might want to say 'Anne won't eat before she is due to go to physiotherapy sessions. In my experience this has always meant that she is distressed in some way.' The phrase 'in my experience' indicates that this is an interpretation. Or you can be much more direct:

Fact: Every Friday afternoon when I bring Mike home from school he is wild. He rushes around so much that it is almost impossible to communicate with him for a good hour. He has only slowed down to a pace that makes it possible to enjoy being with him by Saturday late morning.

My interpretation: Something at school or on the way home must be getting him really angry because that's what he does when he is angry.

If our child has only unintentional communication then, as one of the people who knows the child best, our interpretation as well as our observations may well be vital and will almost certainly be welcomed by a social worker.

What if I'm not really sure yet?

We may not feel sure enough of what is going on to go straight to a social worker. In this event it may be really helpful to talk to someone in our network of friends. We must exercise a little caution, however, if we have a strong sense that abuse may be taking place in an institutional setting. Talking to other parents with children in the same institution as a first step could lead to chaos. It is probably not advisable unless one of them has already been sharing their own concerns with us, or we have a very strong relationship with one of them. In this case, or when there is a professional we already value as a good listener and thinker, it may be best to talk things over with them first. They may help us to pick out a pattern, or find a way of monitoring the situation until the pattern becomes clearer, or suggest other possible causes for our child's behaviour.

Of course, if we are not satisfied with the response we get from any particular professional, we can try another. As a parent or carer of a disabled child there should be at least one other, amongst the many involved with our children, whose opinion we trust and with whom we have a good relationship.

If we, or the person in whom we confide, come up with a non-abuse explanation of the signs and indicators that have been worrying us, it is important to do something new to try to deal with the supposed cause. If the child's behaviour then returns to normal, we can put abuse out of our minds. If, however, it carries on as before, or gets worse, we need to take our concerns further.

For example, we may decide that in all probability, the behaviour that has been worrying us so much may have been caused by the death of the family pet. Our child may not have appeared to react very much at the time and this may have made us feel that perhaps the pet hadn't been as important as we thought. If, on asking the child if they are missing the pet there is a flood of tears, or a tantrum, it may indicate that in fact this was the problem. Allowing more talk about it with or around the child, and perhaps discussions about replacing the pet, may do the trick and our child's behaviour may settle down again. If not, we might return reluctantly to our concerns about abuse.

What if my child tells me about abuse?

Most child abuse is picked up through signs and indicators – which reflects both on the power to silence children held by most perpetrators of abuse, and on common failures to create dependable and open lines of communication with our children. It is unusual for non-disabled children to disclose that they have been abused, and even rarer for disabled children to do so.

Nevertheless disclosures do sometimes happen even amongst children with limited vocabularies or communication skills. In fact, such is the allegiance that often builds up between disabled children within institutions, that a child who has more communication skills will often disclose on behalf of another. So we must be alert for statements that tell us something untoward is going on, and never brush aside comments that seem bald or unlikely, just because they are not expressed in ways that we can readily interpret. It may take a skilled investigator to work out exactly what the child means without spoiling the chance of successful legal action (even as parents we need to avoid leading questions like 'Has your teacher been hitting you?'), but if we have listened carefully and become concerned, that is enough to proceed with. We certainly should not probe for any more information than the child has already given freely, or try to get them to repeat it on tape. All such actions interfere with the proper procedures and can lead to the failure, rather than success of the case. Anyway, children often give a little information first, to guage the reaction, and then more later if they feel safe enough. In the event of a child giving a lot of information, we would do well to take notes of exactly what they are saying – in their own words – and any emotions which accompany it. This will both serve to reassure the child that we are taking them seriously, and help any investigation that might follow.

Gerrilyn Smith lists these six points which are generally considered to be absolutely necessary to give the maximum assistance to any child who has told about abuse:

You want the child to know (a) that they were right to tell; (b) that you believe them; (c) that you will help them sort it out; (d) that the abuser was wrong to do that; (e) that it was not their fault and (f) that you are sorry that it happened to them.[1]

All these apply as much to our disabled children as to any others. However, if you are a carer, even a foster carer, it is safer in terms of the legal processes, not to state explicitly that you believe the child. In his case you simply make it clear to the child through your behaviour that you are taking what is said very seriously. This is because parents to whom children have disclosed are rarely called as witnesses, whereas employees may be. In court, a defence barrister may destroy a child's case by saying that since a worker told a child they believed them, that worker was making assumptions and encouraging the child to continue with something that may not have been the truth. It has to be said that to lay people this is frustrating, but that's how the law operates and it is important not to place any unnecessary obstacles to justice in the child's path.

Certainly, if our children have communicated somehow that they (or another) have been abused, apart from reassuring them that they were right to tell, it is critical that we avoid any comment or even facial expression that suggests we don't or can't believe them. Children are very sensitive to these signals in such difficult situations, and are easily put off by them.

Sometimes believing our children is easier, sometimes it is harder. When the child claims that it is one of the few people we really trusted who is hurting them, our feelings can threaten to overwhelm a rational response. We have to remind ourselves that when it comes to sexual abuse in particular, perpetrators will have carefully built that position of trust, so in a very real sense it is less surprising than if the allegations are made against someone we hardly know. Yet we may be thrown into a state of real shock. In this case we need to take time to compose ourselves. We will need to be calm enough not to be conveying any sense of anger, which our children could imagine is directed at them. We also need to have arranged our own sources of support (people who will act on their belief in both us and our children), so that we can in turn make our children feel more secure.

Who do we tell if we are fairly certain our child is being abused?

We must put our children's need to know what is happening, or about to happen, first. If we are worried that something abusive may have been happening to them, or of course if they let us know that abuse has taken place, it is important that we explain to them that we are going to tell some people who should be able to sort it out and make sure it doesn't happen again. If our child should react to this with extreme fear, or clam up, then we should not be put off. Indeed it should redouble our determination because it may well mean that the child has been threatened with some dreadful consequence of telling. If they *do* react like this we can do a lot worse than acknowledge that what we have said has obviously made them very frightened. We can at least reassure them that we can guess that someone has threatened them and, whilst that person may not really have meant what they said, we will take great care to prevent them from carrying out any of their threats.

Personally I don't think we should minimise the threat. We should not say things like, 'Oh you needn't worry about that, they'd never really do it', because this undermines the child still further. Rather we should acknowledge how seriously the child took the threat, otherwise, no matter how unlikely *we* believe the threat to be, the child will remain frightened. Reassurance is very different from dismissing fears.

We may or may not get the child's agreement to proceed. It would be painful not to, but we could proceed anyway, and hope that the process is sufficiently supportive that we can gradually win them round. If they say they want us to keep it a secret, or not do anything, we have to be clear with them that this is not possible. The pull is either to agree to not taking it further to reduce the child's fear, or not be truthful with them and pretend we won't when in fact we will. The first is too dangerous and the second too damaging. If a child refuses to say anything more because we won't keep it a secret, then we can encourage them to speak to someone else, or, where physically possible, to ring Childline. (Childline do now have minicoms to create access for deaf children who have the ability to use them.) Obviously some of us will not have the option of seeking our children's agreement, but nevertheless I am sure it is helpful to tell them that we think someone may be doing something bad to them and that we are going to try to put a stop to it.

When we are feeling calm enough to listen to our child properly, it is essential that we stress that whatever happened was not their fault. This is because perpetrators nearly always justify their actions by blaming the child . . . 'What do you expect, lying there looking at me like that?' Or 'You got what you deserved, behaving like that', or 'Children like you have to be taught a lesson.' Often the piece going with it will be along the lines of 'Just be thankful I don't tell your mother/father, because they'd kill you if they found out.' Anyway, it is in the nature of young children's thinking in particular, to assume that all that happens to them, good or bad, is a direct result of their own behaviour. So children who have been abused need an enormous amount of reassurance, repeated many times and often over a long period, that what happened is entirely the responsibility of the perpetrator. This is true even if the child was being very difficult at the time.

When we tell our children that we will help them sort the problem out, we must be honest and acknowledge to them that it might be a long, and sometimes difficult, process. If the abuse has taken place in an institution the child will almost certainly be fearful of reprisals, and we would be very wrong either to overlook that possibility, or to minimise it, even though any named member of staff should immediately be suspended from duty. The child will need to be party to thorough discussions about how reprisals might be avoided and what can be done if they should happen.

Next, as parents (other carers have a duty to inform parents first unless they have any suspicions that the abuse may be taking place at home), if we think the abuse has taken place within an institution, or perhaps between home and that place, we can contact the person in charge. They should take us very seriously and act promptly and decisively, involving and informing us at all points. If any of this does not happen, and we can't make it happen, then there is every reason to take it to Social Services.

As carers we should have a written procedure to follow. If you are reading this prior to any concern, but have never seen a copy of your organisation's Child Protection policy and procedures, ask for one to be made available. If we have informed parents that we have concerns, we can offer to help them take it forward, and we must monitor to ensure that the right steps are being taken – or at least that the whole thing isn't just dropped. If the parents are in any way evasive, or aggressive, it is important that we alert others. It is possible to contact the child's head teacher, or go straight to Social Services. Obviously, if we have any fears that the child is being abused within the family, it is safest to go straight to someone like a head teacher, or the named teacher for Child Protection; if it is a health provision, the Child Protection Nurse, if you work for social services then your manager should be able to tell you which duty desk to contact.

We can move straight to contacting our local Social Services duty desk or the Police Child Protection Team. It is certainly better than nothing, but they would probably have to work their way backwards to those professionals I have mentioned anyway, when the abuse is suspected to have taken place outside of the family home.

If we do contact a social worker, we tell that person who we are, and that we have concerns that the child may have been abused. Then they will want to know basic information like names, address, date of birth and so on. They will go on to ask for other information (particularly the things that we have written down about signs and indicators) to help them decide whether or not this should indeed be passed on as a child protection concern. This is where we need to be careful. There are questions the social worker may *not* ask, because of inexperience with disabled children, that are vital to understanding why we think the child may be being abused. We must ensure we give them such information, even if they don't ask.

For example, we may think that it is obvious that any child with severe cerebral palsy needs intimate care, which puts them at risk, but this may not even register with the social worker unless we say so. Having explained the signs that led us to suspect abuse, or of course any statement the child has made, we may have to be very specific: 'My child can feed herself, but she has to be bathed, toileted and dressed and I don't even know all the people who are doing it for her.'

The best way to go about all this is by remembering (if you are not disabled yourself) how much you knew about disability issues before the child came along, and therefore working out what the social worker may need to learn. If you are disabled, you will have stumbled against incredible ignorance so often that you are probably well used to having to start at the very beginning. Undoubtedly social workers vary enormously as to their own personal contact with disability and training on the subject. As we talk to the social worker, we will probably detect how much they know, but it is certainly better to risk offending someone who does know by giving them too much information, than to leave out things that may make or break the social worker's understanding that this really is a child protection issue.

What next?

All too often, sadly, our referrals do not get taken forward as a child protection case. If this happens we can refer again, requesting contact with a team manager, rather than just a duty social worker. Otherwise we can refer to the Police Child Protection Team, explaining what has happened so far and why we are still concerned. In this case we should expect the Social Services to be drawn back into the situation again because the two agencies are supposed to work closely together. However, following this different referral route might produce a better outcome.

In any case, it is advisable to keep a written record of everyone you have spoken to, and of course copies of all letters, with dates and times. This is important so that if things do go wrong, someone will have all the information available as to when, where and with whom it went wrong, and can act accordingly to set it right.

If a child protection case conference is called

The case conference exists to reach a decision about what should happen – and when – to ensure a child's safety and can request a fuller assessment of the situation if it is thought that the picture is inadequate at that point. It decides whether or not to place a child's name on a Child Protection Register.

Parents and the child are usually invited to attend a case conference, although this varies from area to area, except in unusual circumstances. For example, the child may wish to attend but the parent is the alleged abuser and the child does not want to be in the same room. If you are a carer, and you made the original referral, you have every right to be able to attend; if you work in your own home, you can contact Social Services and state that you would like the name of the person chairing the case conference and a way of contacting them to ask permission to attend. If you are a worker in an institution, you can ask your manager to contact the Chairperson of the case conference. But this would only really be appropriate if you made the referral yourself; and have information which you think will help the conference to understand what may have happened to the child, or guide their decisions. It is not appropriate if you just want to know the outcome.

Children are invited if it is thought that this will be helpful for them. And where the child in question is disabled, the number of other people invited can be quite large because many different professionals may have something useful to contribute. So a speech and language therapist might be asked along to help everyone understand the child's communication methods, or to throw light on anything the child may have already communicated. An occupational therapist or a physiotherapist may attend to help the conference understand the implications for a child of the use of equipment or exercises or restraints. And so on. There will almost always be a paediatrician and/or GP who is invited to discuss physical signs and indicators, a representative from the school and someone from the police.

When we are attending case conferences, it is a good idea to have written down in advance anything we think will help, keeping to what we know about the child and any concerns, signs or indicators that we have noted. With all these professionals present, it can be quite intimidating, so it is wise to ask the Chair of the case conference to photocopy what we have written and give each person attending a copy. That way, if we do feel uneasy about speaking at the time, we can be sure our information reaches the right people. As a parent, or someone who looks after the child for significant periods of time – providing foster care or respite in the home – we should automatically be asked to speak at the conference. However, if we give only a few hours' care a week, that might not happen.

Any efficient Social Services will by this point have given us information about what might follow, and what to expect, if we are the child's parents. If we are not, but we have contributed something important to the case conference, we have a right to be kept informed of the decisions that have been made. Unfortunately, workers such as respite care workers from institutions often find that they make a referral and then they hear absolutely nothing. This is not acceptable and managers and Social Services can be badgered for information because, after all, it is in the child's best interests for us to have some sense of what is happening if we are to continue to work well with them.

Recovery

It is really important to remind ourselves that children *can* and *do* recover from the effects of abuse. Despite all the damage it can do, our mental processes are obstinately in favour of survival and recovery. Children may use any of hundreds of strategies to survive and these should be recognised and honoured by others, even if society usually frowns upon them (like trying to get attention all the time), or finds them difficult to handle (like rushing around non-stop). They are all strategies to help the child feel safe, or to try to get a message across. Children, and adults for that matter, are not going to give

these up easily until someone has been able to understand their purpose and congratulate the child on their
efforts.

Why do I say that our mental processes are *obstinately*
in favour of survival and recovery? Even when an
experience has been so painful that we have blotted it
out, pushed it back into the deepest recesses of our
minds, if there are truly safe conditions, even twenty or
thirty years later, we will find ourselves bringing the
memories back out into the light of day; slowly and
painfully perhaps, but out they will come and recovery,
as opposed to pure survival, will have begun.

Clearly then, if we communicate to our children our
belief in them – in their goodness, strength and so on; if
they can trust us to listen to them respectfully; if they
know we will love them whatever emerges, we can help
them reach the recovery stage much more quickly. We
too, as parents or carers, may have a recovery process to
pursue. We may well have enormous feelings of guilt; we
may fear a repetition; we may feel great anger towards
the perpetrator or others who we feel, or perhaps know,
allowed it to happen. It is important for the child that we
deal with these feelings, partly so that we don't impose
them on the child in any way, and partly so that the
damage we have sustained emotionally doesn't get in the
way of their recovery.

Frankly, it is brought home to me time and time again
that most of our children are tough as old boots, when it
comes down to it. If we behave as if we have faith that
we and they can survive and recover and carry some
treasures of insight, sensitivity and wisdom out of it, then
that is what will happen.

Regretfully, it must be said that if our child uses non-
verbal communication, or has a very limited vocabulary,
we do have to be prepared for the likelihood of our
child's case never reaching court. Sometimes the police

have been very supportive up to this point, but it is then taken out of their hands by the Crown Prosecution Service. Even with recent improvements, our judicial system mitigates against all child witnesses and such is the legal dependency on the spoken or written word, that children such as those mentioned are not likely to be deemed 'competent witnesses'.

This is often not as catastrophic as it first appears. One reason is that the court process can be too much for a child, and add to the trauma. The second is that, when the abuse took place in an institution, we can institute civil proceedings which will at least lead to the dismissal of that member of staff for gross misconduct. If the abuser was a family member or the abuse took place in the home, then that person can be removed.

It is true that most of us would prefer to see justice to be done, and the child often needs that affirming result. But the level of proof needed in civil proceedings is less exacting than in criminal courts, so it is possible that the outcome will be better. It should be stressed that the care and attention to detail that has been put forward as necessary throughout this chapter, will be no less necessary or helpful in civil proceedings.

Having said this, there have been precedents set in the criminal court. For example, one perpetrator was convicted after seven deaf boys testified against him using British Sign Language. There have also been one or two successes involving children with learning difficulties, so we should start out with a positive attitude. Professional awareness in general, and legal awareness in particular, are beginning to improve and no doubt will continue to do so.

This chapter is all about taking our own concerns seriously, recognising signs and indicators and, of course, disclosures. I have emphasised how essential it is to write down our worries and record anything suspicious. We will be overjoyed if we can throw these things away because they did not turn out to be of any consequence, but we can make protecting our child – and getting justice for them – much more difficult if we try to depend on our memories.

Nevertheless I should also acknowledge that trying to ensure that children are protected – let alone trying to secure justice for them – is a stressful and often long-winded business. We will need good, long-term support from professionals, family and friends. We should not attempt to go it alone, for that is nigh on impossible both emotionally and practically.

Despite all the difficulties we may face, getting it right for our children must be our top priority – and presumably that is why you have read this book.

Endword

I do hope that on balance what you have read has felt supportive. I'm sure that some of it will have been painful to read and even shocking, though the aim was never to shock for the sake of it. Large parts of the book are, in effect, guides to good parenting of disabled children which, at the same time, promotes protective skills and behaviours. As such, I hope that the book might have helped provide you with some fresh ideas.

I would love to think that it has given some of you new insight into the children in your care, and has boosted your enthusiasm for working constructively with them, even though you may have an increased awareness of the risks they face.

Whilst there are some current social processes which worry me, and which are taking us backwards rather than forwards in terms of quite fundamental disability rights, there is much that is helpful and encouraging. Following the publication of the *ABCD* pack, huge numbers of professionals have now been trained in at least some aspects of protecting our children from abuse, and thinking and practices are being pushed forwards all the time. Local authorities are also being encouraged to improve their policies and procedures, as are schools and charities.

We can both take heart from this and play our part in it. Certainly I have written this book in the hope that parents and carers will be better equipped to protect disabled children, but also in the hope that we can thereby advance the child protection system towards proper and effective inclusion of all our children.

Notes

Foreword

1. SB Crosse, E Kaye and AC Ratnofsky, 'A Report on the Maltreatment of Children with Disabilities', National Center on Child Abuse and Neglect, Washington, 1993.
2. Ruth Bailey, 'Prenatal Testing and the Prevention of Impairment', in Jenny Morris, ed, *Encounters with Strangers*, The Women's Press, London, 1996.

Introduction

1. National Commission of Enquiry into Child Protection, 'Childhood Matters', 1997.
2. 'Working Together Under the Children Act 1989', Department of Health.
3. In Munchausen's syndrome itself, the adult presents themselves to the doctor with false symptoms. In Munchausen's syndrome by proxy, a parent presents their child to doctors with an illness or symptoms that may have been artificially produced. Sometimes children have not only received medication but may have had several operations before suspicions are aroused.

4. Ruth Marchant and Marcus Page, *Bridging the Gap*, NSPCC, 1992.
5. David Finkelhor, *Child Sexual Abuse: New Theory and Research*, The Free Press, New York, 1984.
6. Gerrilyn Smith, *The Protector's Handbook*, The Women's Press, London, 1995.

Chapter One: Self-Image

1. Ellen Kuzwayo, *Call Me Woman*, The Women's Press, London, 1985.
2. Merry Cross, 'Merry', in Jo Campling, ed, *Images of Ourselves*, Routledge & Kegan Paul, London, 1985.
3. *The Best of Both Worlds*, from EYTARN (see Resources List page 201).
4. David Hevey, *The Creatures That Time Forgot: Photography and Disability Imagery*, Routledge, London, 1992.
5. Michael Hull, *Touching the Rock*, Society for Promoting Christian Knowledge, London, 1990.
6. Micheline Mason, 'Micheline', in *Images of Ourselves*, op. cit.
7. Jenny Morris, *Pride Aainst Prejudice*, The Women's Press, London, 1991.
8. David Hevey, op. cit.

Chapter Two: Communicating with our Children

1. Sarah Beazley and Michele Moore. *Deaf Children, Their Families and Professionals: Dismantling Barriers*, David Fulton, London, 1995.
2. Margaret Kennedy, *You Choose*, National Deaf Children's Society, 1989.
3. Christopher Nolan, *The Eye of the Clock: The Life Story of Christopher Nolan*, Delta, London, 1989.

Chapter Three: Intimate Care

1. Sally French, 'Out of Sight, Out of Mind' in Jenny Morris, ed, *Encounters with Strangers*, op. cit.

2. Ruth Marchant in the Reader from *The ABCD Pack: Abuse and Children who are Disabled*, Department of Health, 1993, available from the NSPCC National Training Centre, Leicester.
3. This statistic is taken from some unpublished research, 'Having a Say', conducted at Chailey Heritage.
4. Jacqui Saradjian, *Women Who Sexually Abuse Children: From Research to Clinical Practice*, Wiley, Chichester, 1996.
5. Ruth Marchant and Marcus Page, *Bridging the Gap*, op. cit.

Chapter Four: Sexuality and Sexual Relationships
1. Nasa Begum, 'Doctor, Doctor' in Jenny Morris, ed, *Encounters with Strangers*, op. cit.
2. Ruth Bailey, op. cit.
3. Dick Sobsey, *Violence and Abuse in the Lives of People with Disabilities: The End of Silent Acceptance?*, Paul H Brookes, New York, 1994.
4. See *Turning Points*, a resource pack for communicating with children, especially the sections on challenging behaviour, trust, sexuality and relationships, rights, and safety. NSPCC, 1997.

Chapter Five: Pots of Professionals
1. J Swain, V Finkelstein and S French, *Disabling Barriers, Enabling Environments*, Oxford University Press, 1993.
2. Ruth Marchant and Merry Cross in *ABCD* Reader, op. cit.
3. Parents with Attitude, *Let our Children Be*, collated by Pippa Murray and Jill Penman and available c/o 44 Cowlishaw Road, Sheffield, S11 8XF.

Chapter Six: Medical Intervention
1. Helen Westcott, *Abuse of Children and Adults with Disabilities*, NSPCC, 1993.

Chapter Seven: Our Children in School

1. Helen Westcott and Merry Cross, *Towards Ending the Abuse of Disabled Children*, Venture Press, Birmingham, 1996.
2. M Mason and R Reiser, *All Together Better Training Pack*, Hobsons Publishing, London.
3. Ruth Marchant and Merry Cross in *ABCD* Reader, op. cit.
4. Sally French, op. cit.

Chapter Eight: Signs and Indicators of Abuse in Disabled Children

1. Gerrilyn Smith, *The Protector's Handbook*, op. cit. Also in *ABCD* Reader, op. cit.
2. SB Crosse, E Kaye and AC Ratnofsky, op. cit.
3. Ruth Marchant and Marcus Page, *Bridging the Gap*, op. cit.

Chapter Nine: What to Do if you Suspect Abuse

1. Gerrilyn Smith, *The Protector's Handbook*, op. cit.

Appendix I

Everywoman's bill of assertive rights

The following is useful for disabled boys as well as girls, despite the title. Everything in ordinary print is fom *New Assertive Woman* by Lynn Bloom, Karen Coburn and John Pearlman Bell. Everything in italics has been added by Saadia Neilson and myself.

1. The right to be treated with respect *at all times, by all people, including all professionals.*
2. The right to have and express your own feelings and opinions, *including all negative feelings like anger, boredom, upset and fear, even when other people think they are being nice to you!*
3. The right to be listened to *(whatever form that listening may have to take)* and taken seriously.
4. The right to your own priorities, *especially in relation to which self-help skills you want to develop and when.*
5. *A way of communicating No, preferably different ones for different levels. That is, one for No and at*

least one other for DEFINITELY NOT ON ANY ACCOUNT.
The right to say NO without feeling guilty.
6. The right to ask for what you want.
7. The right to ask for information from professionals, *especially about any kinds of treatment or equipment they are proposing.*
8. The right to make mistakes *and therefore the opportunity to make mistakes.*
9. The right to choose not to assert yourself.
10. *The right to dignity at all times.*

The next set comes from *When I say No I Feel Guilty* (Manuel J Smith, Bantam Books, 1975) again with additions by Saadia Neilson and myself in italics.

A bill of assertive rights
1. You have the right to judge your own behaviour, thoughts and emotions and to take responsibility for their initiation and consequences upon yourself.
2. You have the right to offer no reasons or excuses for justifying your behaviour.
3. You have the right to judge if you are responsible for finding solutions to other people's problems, *and the right to decide what is their problem, and not yours! (For example, if someone can't understand you despite your best efforts, and because they are not really trying, that is* THEIR *problem).*
4. You have the right to change your mind.
5. You have the right to make mistakes – and be responsible for them.
6. You have the right to say, 'I don't know.'
7. You have the right to be independent of the good will of others before coping with them. *In other words, we should not criticise ourselves* OR ALLOW OURSELVES TO BE CRITICISED *for failing to cope with bad behaviour from someone on whom we are dependent.*

8. You have the right to be 'illogical' in making decisions.
9. You have the right to say, 'I don't understand.'
10. You have the right to say, 'I don't care.'
11. *You have the right to take risks.*
12. *You have the right to question all decisions taken about your body.*
13. *You have the right to refuse all kinds of treatment and equipment until and unless you have enough information to satisfy you that the end result will be worth whatever you have to go through.*
14. *You have the right to decide how much, or what kind of help you do and do not need at any time.*
15. *You have the right to ask for help or refuse it without feeling guilty.*
16. *You have the right to complain to those in authority when you are treated badly, without fear of punishment.*
17. *YOU HAVE THE RIGHT TO BE PROUD OF YOURSELF EXACTLY AS YOU ARE, WITHOUT ANY CHANGES.*

These do need to be worked through slowly, and with as much explanation or examples as necessary. Many of these will feel very relevant to us as parents and carers, and on the other hand, some will feel very challenging when we imagine our children following them!

Appendix II

Index of suspicion of sexual abuse
Gerrilyn Smith

Key: Red   = high probability of sexual abuse occurring
      Green = sexual abuse possibly occurring
      Blue = one hypothesis amongst many

Under 5
Red
Disclosure
Genital injuries
VD
Vivid details of sexual
  activity (such as penetra-
  tion, oral sex, ejaculation)
compulsive masturbation
  (contextually abnormal)
Sexual drawings
Sexualised play, with
  explicit acts

5-12 years
Red
Pregnancy/abortion
Disclosure
Genital injuries
VD
Explicit sexual stories/poems
Exposing themselves
Masturbation in contex-
  tually inappropriate
  fashion
'Promiscuity'
Suicide attempts
Running away
Alcohol and drug abuse
Offending/abusing
Gender identity difficulties

12-16 years
Red
Disclosures
Genital injuries
Self-mutilation of
  breasts/genitals
Pregnancy (under 14)
VD (under 14)
Prostitution
Sexual Offending
Gender identity difficulties

Green
Person specific fear
Nightmares
Chronic genito-urinary
  infections
Soreness of genitals/bottom
Fears of specific situations:
  fear of being bathed
  fear of being changed
  fear of being put to bed

Green
Arson
Soreness of genitals/bottom
Chronic genito/urinary
  infections
Obsessive washing
Depression
Bedwetting/enuresis
Anal incontinence/
  encopresis
Anorexia
Glue sniffing
Nightmares
Truanting
Unexplained large sums of
  money/gifts

Green
Sexual boasting/stories/
  jokes
VD (over 14)
Pregnancy (over 14)
Rebellious against men
  (specific gender)
Drug and alcohol abuse
Suicide attempts
Self-mutilation
Truanting
Running away
Hysterical symptoms
Obsessional washing
Psychotic episodes
HIV (though no necessarily a
  sexually transmitted virus)

Blue
Developmental regression
Hostile/aggressive
  behaviour
Pyschosomatic condition
HIV

Blue
Abdominal pains
Developmental regression
Peer problems
HIV
School problems
Psychosomatic conditions

Blue
Depression
Anorexia
Refusing to attend school
Peer problems
Authority problems
Delinquency
Psychosomatic conditions

Possible signs of emotional abuse

- physical, mental and emotional development delay or disturbance
- admission of punishment which appears excessive
- over-reaction to mistakes
- sudden speech disorders
- fear of new situations
- inappropriate emotional responses to stressful situations
- neurotic behaviour
  (eg rocking, hair-twisting, thumb-sucking)
- self-mutilation
- fear of parents being contacted
- extremes of passivity or aggression
- drug/solvent abuse
- chronic running away
- compulsive stealing
- scavenging for food or clothes
- enuresis/encopresis (bedwetting/soiling)

Possible signs of physical abuse

- unexplained injuries or burns, particularly if they are recurrent
- Improbable excuses gven to explain injuries
- refusal to discuss injuries
- untreated injuries
- admission of punishment which appears excessive
- fear of parents being contacted
- withdrawal from physical contact
- flinching at sudden movements
- arms and legs kept covered in hot weather
- fear of returning home
- fear of medical help
- self-destructive tendencies
- aggression towards others
- chronic running away

Possible signs of neglect

- constant hunger
- poor personal hygiene
- constant tiredness
- poor state of clothing
- emaciation
- frequent lateness or non-attendance at school
- untreated medical problems
- destructive tendencies
- low self-esteem
- neurotic behaviour (eg rocking, hair twisting, thumb-sucking)
- no social relationships
- chronic running away
- compulsive stealing
- scavenging for food or clothes

Resource list

'Let's Talk about Sex' and 'More about Sex' and 'Say No to Bullying' Free Leaflets for children. There are a few direct references to Spina Bifida, but the content would be suitable for children with most impairments. These are available from:
Association for Spina Bifida and Hydrocephalus (ASBAH)
ASBAH House
42 Park Road
Peterborough
PE1 2UQ
Tel: 01773 555988

Asian People with Disabilities Alliance
Disability Alliance Centre
Central Middlesex Hospital
Old Refectory
Acton Lane
London
NW10 7NS
Tel: 0181 961 6773

Blissymbolics Communication Resource Centre (UK)
South Glamorgan Institute of Higher Education
Western Avenue
Llandaft
CF5 2YB
Tel: 01222 537770

**British Council of Organisations of Disabled People
(BCODP)**
Litchurch Plaza
Litchurch Lane
Derbyshire
DE24 8AA
Tel: 01332 295551

British Deaf Association (BDA)
Head Office
38 Victoria Place
Carlisle
CA1 1HU
Tel and text: 01228 548844

Chailey's Charter of Children's Rights; Guidelines for
Good Practice in Intimate Care (this is for staff, not
parents); Guidelines for Working with Children with
Difficult Behaviour; Chailey Communication System are
all available from:
Chailey Heritage
North Chailey
Nr. Lewes
East Sussex
BN8 4EQ
Tel: 01825 722112

Early Years Training Anti-racist Network (EYTARN)
PO Box 28
Wallesey
L45 9NP

Makaton Vocabulary Project
31 Firwood Drive
Camberley
Surrey
GU15 3QD

National Association for the Protection from Sexual Abuse of Adults and Children with Learning Disabilities (NAPSAC)
Department of Learning Disabilities
E Floor
South Block
University Hospital
Nottingham
NG27 2UH
Tel: 0115 970 1598

Also available from this department: 'Sex Education for Students with Learning Disabilities: A Resource List', compiled by Ann Craft.

Parentability
c/o The National Childbirth Trust
Alexandra House
Oldham Terrace
Acton
London
W3 6NH

People Potential, Jean and Ken Westmacott (for making your own equipment)
Plum Cottage
Hattingley
Hants
GU34 SNQ
Tel: 01420 563741

Royal National Institute for the Blind (RNIB)
224 Great Portland Street
London
W1N 6AA
Tel: 0171 388 1266

Sigsymbols
Ailsa Cregan
Coles Green School
Dollis Hill Lane
London
NW2
Tel: 0181 450 2550

'Sex and Your Child with a Disability' is one of fourteen leaflets (mostly written for adults) available at 50p from SPOD. Also available from this organisation or ASBAH is a book, *Sex for Young People with Spina Bifida and Cerebral Palsy*, available at £2.50 from:
The Association to Aid the Sexual and Personal Relationships of People with a Disability (SPOD)
286 Camden Road
London
N7 0BJ
Tel: 0171 607 8851

Lamplugh Trust (for self-defence leaflets and courses)
14 East Sheen
London
SW14 8AS

Voluntary Council for Disabled Children
8 Wakely Street
London
EC1V 7QE

If you want to consult Merry Cross, you may do so
(letters only)
c/o The Department of Psychology
Westminster University
309 Regent Street
London
W1R 8AZ

Other useful books

Sex Education for Visually Impaired Children with Additional Disabilities, from RNIB

Pat Filton, *Listen to Me: Communicating the Needs of People with Profound Intellectual and Multiple Disabilities*, Jessica Kingsley, London, 1994

Lois Keith, *Think About People who use Wheelchairs*, Belitha Press, London, 1998

Jenny Morris, *Still Missing Report Volume I: The Experience of Disabled Children and Young People Living Away From Their Families*, Who Cares Trust, 1998

—, *Still Missing Report Volume II: The Experience of Disabled Children and Young People Living Away From Their Families*, Who Cares Trust, 1998

Tom Shakespeare, Cath Gillespie-Sells and Dominic Davies, *Sexual Politics of Disability: Untold Desires*, Cassell, London, 1997

Valerie Sinason, *Understanding Your Disabled Child*, Tavistock Press, London, 1994

Peter White, *Think About People who are Blind*, Belitha Press, London, 1998

Maggie Woolley, *Think About People who are Deaf*, Belitha Press, London, 1998

Training packs (designed for workers, but which institutions may not be aware of)

Sex in context, Ann Craft and Caroline Downes, available from:

Pavilion Publishing
8 St George's Place
Brighton E Sussex
BN1 4ZZ

Disability – Identity Sexuality and Relationhips, available from:
Department of Health and Social Welfare
The Open University
Walton Hall
Milton Keynes
MK7 6AA

The Women's Press is Britain's leading women's publishing house. Established in 1978, we publish high-quality fiction and non-fiction from outstanding women writers worldwide. Our exciting and diverse list includes literary fiction, detective novels, biography and autobiography, health, women's studies, handbooks, literary criticism, psychology and self-help, the arts, our popular Livewire Books series for young women and the bestselling annual *Women Artists Diary* featuring beautiful colour and black-and-white illustrations from the best in contemporary women's art.

If you would like more information about our books or about our mail order book club, please send an A5 sae for our latest catalogue and complete list to:

The Sales Department
The Women's Press Ltd
34 Great Sutton Street
London EC1V 0DX
Tel: 0171 251 3007
Fax: 0171 608 1938

Livewire Books for Young Women

Lois Keith
A Different Life

Libby Starling can't wait for the school trip to come. But what is she going to wear? Will Cleo ignore her again? And what about quiet, confident Jesse – will he notice her at last?

A week later, it is impossible for Libby to believe that this was all she had to worry about. Because after the school trip, everything has changed.

After a swim in the sea, Libby becomes mysteriously ill. Everyone seems to know what's best for her – doctors, physiotherapists, parents, the headteacher. Libby realises that she must choose what is important to her now. She learns how to be strong, and, with the help of those who love her, she starts to live a new, different life . . .

'As with the best of novels, I did not want this story to end.' *Sunday Times*

'Can be enjoyed by young disabled people and non-disabled people . . . grab a copy, spend some time with lively Elizabeth Starling, and see for yourself.' *DIAL*

'A wonderful book.' *Disability Times*

Young Adult Fiction £5.99
ISBN 0 7043 4946 9

The Women's Press Handbook Series

Gerrilyn Smith
The Protectors' Handbook
Reducing the Risk of Child Sexual Abuse and Helping
Children Recover

How much more effective would we be in working against child
sexual abuse if every adult had the knowledge currently available
only to professionals?

With child sexual abuse now unquestionably widespread, every
adult in contact with children must – and can – be an active
protector. Now, in this unique and essential book, child
psychologist Gerrilyn Smith gives adults all the information and
skills needed to protect children in their day-to-day lives. Drawing
on her many years of professional experience in the field, a wide
range of sources and proven techniques – as well as the
experiences of young survivors themselves – she offers a fully
comprehensive, practical and step-by-step guide to recognising,
reducing the risks, and overcoming the effects of abuse.

From being aware of the many possible signs of abuse to helping
a child confide, from creating the best context for recovery to
finding the most appropriate professional help, this urgently needed,
accessible book is absolutely essential reading for every adult.

Health/Self-help £6.99
ISBN 0 7043 4417 3

Jenny Morris
Pride Against Prejudice
Transforming Attitudes to Disability

A bestseller since its first publication in 1991, *Pride Against Prejudice* is a groundbreaking analysis of the position of disabled women in contemporary society. Examining the nature of prejudice against disabled women, the experience of being different, and ways of fighting back, *Pride Against Prejudice* also explores important specific issues – how institutionalisation can segregate disabled women, the role of charity in undermining disability rights, how traditional feminist views of abortion and prenatal testing help to devalue disabled women's lives and much more. Including powerful personal accounts from disabled women, and providing a wide-ranging overview of current and historical perspectives on the quality of disabled women's lives, this excellent book is argued with energy, authority and conviction. It is a major work on the most important social and political issue today.

'Contributions from eight disabled women lend colour and substance to many of Morris' points. But it is Morris' conviction and anger which keep this book alive. I recommend this book to anyone.' *Link*

'Looks at every prejudice that confronts the independent and meaningful lives of disabled people. Recommended reading for everyone.' *Disability News*

'A book long overdue.' *Community Care*

'A powerful polemic.' *Observer*

'Informative, uplifting and empowering.' *Northern Star*

Health/Disability £7.99
ISBN 0 7043 4286 3

Anne Finger
Past Due
A Story of Disability, Pregnancy and Birth

Should a physically disabled woman be supported in her desire to have a child — moreover, to have the homebirth of her choice?

In this moving, deeply felt book, writer Anne Finger — herself physically disabled by polio — explores the complexity of disability and reproductive rights through an engrossing account of her own pregnancy and childbirth.

This is an unforgettable story of maternal determination and love which also newly illuminates the implications of a 'woman's right to choose'.

Health/Pregnancy/Disability £6.95
ISBN 0 7043 4291 X

Judith Arcana
Every Mother's Son
The Role of Mothers in the Making of Men

'The boys: how can they withstand the pressure? How
can they say no to the gift of power? How can they turn a
deaf ear, a blind eye, to television, to the toys – to the
girly magazines? And what about the responsibility for all
of that? Must mothers of sons run interference on the
whole damn culture for our sons?'

How can a mother care lovingly for a small boy, yet avoid
reinforcing the examples he receives from all around him? How can
she challenge male stereotypes, and at the same time fit him to
survive in the world in which we live? Can our sons grow up to
be our friends? Judith Arcana, author of the much-loved bestseller
Our Mothers' Daughters, faced these questions with her own son,
and has drawn on the diary she kept then, as well as on
interviews with other women, to write this moving, honest and
thought-provoking book.

'Truly wonderful.' Phyllis Chesler

Parenting/Psychology £8.99
ISBN 0 7043 3916 1